THE WAY OF PERFECTION

Teresa of Avila

Edited and Mildly Modernized by
HENRY L. CARRIGAN, JR.

PARACLETE PRESS
BREWSTER, MASSACHUSETTS

Library of Congress Cataloging-in-Publication Data

Teresa, of Avila, Saint, 1515–1582.
  [Camino de perfecciíon. English]
  The way of perfection / Teresa of Avila ; edited and mildly mod-
ernized by Henry L. Carrigan, Jr.
        p. cm.
  ISBN 1-55725-248-3 (pbk.)
  1. Perfection–Religious aspects–Catholic Church. 2. God–
Worship and love. I. Carrigan, Henry L., 1954– II. Title.

BX2179.T4 C32 2000
248.8'943–dc21   99-059805

10 9 8 7 6 5 4 3

© 2000 by Paraclete Press
ISBN 1-55725-248-3

Published by Paraclete Press
Brewster, Massachusetts
www.paracletepress.com

Printed in the United States of America.

CONTENTS

INTRODUCTION

In our times, the spiritual writings of Teresa of Avila are very popular. People searching for a spirituality that can be folded into their everyday lives have returned over and over again to Teresa's writings because of their power and their simplicity. Teresa is a steadfast lover of tradition, and her writings often begin by exhorting her readers to pray for the leaders of the Church, for they are the ones who have been instrumental in teaching the doctrines and principles followed by the convents. Her own love of the Church is manifest in her obedience not only to God but to her confessor and to the monastic rules established by earlier reform movements. Although Teresa fashioned these rules to fit her own community, she stressed obedience to the vows of poverty, solitude, and mutual love that were part of her religious community. People seeking simple spiritual answers will not find them in Teresa, but those who are committed to seeking God through a life of prayer and regular spiritual discipline will be delighted with Teresa.

Teresa's greatest virtue is that she acknowledges our humanity and her own. She knows that we yearn to lead spiritual lives but that we often do not have the will or the courage to discipline ourselves to be spiritual. In *The Way of Perfection*, she offers a path that she believes can offer us a way to incorporate our yearning to be spiritual into our everyday lives. If we were to use her exposition of the Lord's Prayer as our devotional material even for six weeks, we would find ourselves immeasurably enriched, and we would probably feel closer to God than we have ever felt. Long before the popular spirituality of today's writers, Teresa showed readers how to make the spiritual part of the everyday.

Biography

Although there are several biographies of Teresa, she provides the details of her young life in her autobiography, *The Life of Saint Teresa of Avila By Herself.* We know from this writing that she loved and respected her father a great deal, that she and her brother were spiritually precocious youngsters who once ran away from home with the hopes of being martyred in Morocco, and that her mother died when she was fourteen. Teresa also provides a detailed overview of her journey from spiritual novitiate at an Augustinian convent, through several illnesses, to her attainment of perfect contemplation and her establishment of the Order of Discalced

(Reformed, barefoot) Carmelites. Teresa also describes in visceral language the visions and raptures that accompanied her experience of inner contemplation.

On March 28, 1515, Teresa Sánchez de Cepeda y Ahumada was born to her father's second wife in the little Castilian town of Avila. Although her family was Christian, her grandfather, Juan Sánchez, of Toledo was Jewish. She was educated as a young woman of her social rank. Teresa's mother taught her at home in the subjects with which she herself was familiar, but this did not include instruction in Latin or the religious classics. In addition to running away with her brother in hopes of attaining martyrdom, she often built little hermitages as a young girl.

When Teresa was fourteen, and her mother died, her reaction was to become enamored of chivalric romances and to immerse herself in worldly things. Her father sent her to a school run by Augustinian nuns when she was sixteen. When she was almost eighteen, Teresa became ill, and her father took her out of the school. Recovering from this illness, she experienced the first step on the way to becoming a Carmelite nun, for she read the letters of Jerome, the fourth-century monk who translated the Bible into Latin (the *Vulgate*) so that ordinary people could have access to it. After reading these letters, she decided to become a nun. At first, her father refused to let her join the convent, but he eventually consented, and, when she was twenty or twenty-one, Teresa entered the Carmelite convent of the Incarnation of Avila.

A year after entering the convent, Teresa became ill again. She experienced symptoms that in the late twentieth century would be associated with an "anxiety attack." She was afflicted with violent attacks of vomiting, heart palpitations, cramps, and partial paralysis. Some interpreters have suspected that these problems were more mental than physical, for during this year Teresa was working hard to achieve perfect contemplation. Others have called Teresa's illness a malignant malaria. Whatever its cause, Teresa left the convent to be treated by her family doctors.

After three years, she returned to the Carmelite convent where she resumed her search for perfect contemplation. The convent itself was very large, with an estimated 140 nuns, and was somewhat relaxed in its adherence to and practice of its rules. Wealthy visitors from the town often visited the convent's parlor, and the nuns were free to leave the convent on a regular basis. During these years, Teresa first practiced the mental prayer that became the foundation of her own spiritual life and her teachings about prayer. Although she at first gave up this practice, she resumed it after her father's death in 1543, and did not give it up again. Between her entrance into the convent at twenty and her inner conversion in 1555 at age forty, Teresa writes that she was "engaged in strife and contention between converse with God and the society of the world." When she was forty, she first read Augustine's *Confessions*. Though she had been educated briefly by Augustinian nuns as a young girl, she had not before been bathed in the waters of Augustine's piety. Her picking up of Augustine coincided with an inner conversion that had occurred as a result of her continuing practice of prayer. In her autobiography, she describes the effect that Augustine has upon her:

> O my Lord, I am amazed that my soul was so stubborn when You had helped me so much. I am frightened by how little I could do by myself and of those attachments that were obstacles to my determination to give myself entirely to God. When I began to read the *Confessions*, I saw myself portrayed there, and I began to commend myself frequently to that glorious saint. When I came to the tale of his conversion, and read how he heard the voice in the garden, it seemed as if the Lord had spoken to me. I felt this way in my heart. For some time, I was dissolved in tears, in great inward affliction and distress. The soul suffers so much, O Lord, when it loses its freedom. It was once its own mistress, but now it endures great torments. I am amazed today that I was ever able to live under such torture. May God, who gave me life to escape from such death, be praised.

After her conversion, Teresa became increasingly dissatisfied with the convent at Avila. Teresa was concerned mainly that the Avila convent did not encourage or honor solitude or poverty, two characteristics that she thought absolutely essential to the lives of those seeking perfect contemplation and union with God. Thus, around 1560, she sought to establish a religious community that would be governed by strict adherence to the rules of solitude and poverty. Although both civil and ecclesiastical authorities opposed her plan, she in 1562 founded the convent of St. Joseph of Avila, which became the model for at least sixteen other houses of the same type. There were thirteen nuns who took vows of poverty and solitude, and they were known by the coarse brown wool habits and leather sandals that they wore as they practiced their rule. The convent's income was provided by monetary offerings and by a program of manual work. The rules of the convent encouraged simple living, including abstinence from meat, and the convent building provided whatever essentials satisfied the basic needs of the sisters. Although Teresa thought of herself as a contemplative, she was as active as any other nun in caring for the convent, taking her turn at sweeping or other manual tasks. When she sought candidates for entrance into the convent, she looked for women who were intelligent and who had good judgment, for she thought that intelligent people could see their shortcomings and be taught ways to overcome them, while narrow-minded people are often so arrogant that they would never see their imperfections.

In the later half of the 1560s, Teresa's pupil, John of the Cross, pushed for a reform of Carmelite monasteries along the same lines that Teresa had pursued with her convent. These Discalced Carmelite friars often provided spiritual direction to the nuns.

Teresa died on October 4, 1582, in Alba de Tormes, as she returned from establishing a convent in Burgos. She was buried in Alba de Tormes. In 1622, she was canonized, and in 1970 she became the first woman saint to be declared a Doctor of the Church.

The Way of Perfection

Teresa wrote *The Way of Perfection* in 1565–1566 to provide instruction in the life of prayer to the sisters of St. Joseph's convent. The book had another purpose as well, though.

Teresa had written her autobiography three years prior to *The Way of Perfection*. Many of the nuns at St. Joseph's probably knew that Teresa had written this earlier book, and although not many had read it, they knew it offered a great deal of insight into the life of prayer and contemplation. However, because the autobiography contained material that in the eyes of the Church's censors and Teresa's confessors was objectionable, they did not want the sisters of St. Joseph to read it. Thus, in her prologue she writes, "A few days ago I was commanded to write an account of my life in which I also dealt with certain matters concerning prayer. It may be that my confessor will not wish you to see that book, so I set down here some of the things that I said in that book as well as other things that seem necessary to me." *The Way of Perfection* incorporates some of Teresa's autobiography, but its primary focus is on the various practices of prayer that lead to perfect contemplation.

In the opening chapter, Teresa provides her reasons for founding the convent at St. Joseph of Avila. She writes that she wants to establish a house where the vows of simplicity, poverty, and solitude will help the sisters achieve union with God. As she looks around her, she sees that what she calls the excesses of the Protestant Reformation are encouraging a new kind of freedom from God's rule for the soul. Teresa condemns the Lutherans as traitors who "send Christ to the Cross again." Teresa also instructs her sisters in this first chapter to seek poverty and "not to pray for worldly things." She contends that she has brought them together in this house so that they may seek God together through their common dedication to the vows they have taken.

The overall structure of the book is fairly simple, but Teresa's exhortation to the life of prayer builds in intensity as the book progresses. Chapters 1–3 discuss the role of the Church in the sisters' education. After her indictment of the Lutherans, she encourages her followers to pray for the theologians and priests of the Church who have done so much in establishing the principles and rules the sisters are following. In chapters 4–15, Teresa discusses the ways that her nuns can prepare themselves fully for a life of perfect contemplation. According to Teresa, the three virtues that will prepare the nuns to achieve this state are love for each other; detachment from one's self, family, and world; and humility. Chapters 16–26 amplify these ideas. Teresa argues that perfect union with the Beloved cannot be attained without constant self-sacrifice. The mystical state that contemplatives achieve is only transitory, and these states simply make the contemplative want to be more virtuous and strive for union in a more fervent way. In these chapters Teresa also discusses other questions like "Is it possible for all souls to attain contemplation?" and "How can a person reach perfection without the experience of contemplation?" She also discusses the various practices of prayer—vocal and mental—and exhorts her followers to imagine Jesus as living in their hearts and as always walking beside them.

In chapters 27–42, Teresa offers her well-known exposition of the Paternoster, the Lord's Prayer. She examines each section, or petition, of the prayer individually and concludes that this prayer provides the way to the fountain of eternal water that she has encouraged her followers to seek. During her examination of the Paternoster, Teresa continues to encourage her sisters to practice the virtues of humility, detachment, and love for one another. There is an extended discussion on the nature of temptations and how we succumb to them, and she exhorts her sisters to love and fear God if they would avoid temptation. Finally, she prays that God will protect His followers from the sins of this world as they seek the peace and joy of God's eternal Kingdom.

Teresa teaches her followers in a simple language that they can understand. Although her theological discussions are founded on complex ideas, she is careful always to use images drawn from everyday life so that the sisters can understand the difficult concepts through Teresa's analogies. She uses a colloquial style to describe not only her own intense mystical experiences but also the life of perfect union that her sisters can expect if they follow her advice. She draws much of her imagery from the relationship between lover and beloved, and she also portrays many of her ecstatic experiences in physical, bodily, and sensual terms. In addition, she is often self-effacing in her remarks. She continually contends that she knows very little about a certain form of prayer, or that she is sure that the Lord must have overcome a good deal of repulsion to use her in the glorious way He is doing as an instrument to teach others. Teresa emphasizes her own unworthiness as she teaches about the way that God has taught her the path of perfection. She often emphasizes her personal experience as an example of the way to pursue perfect union. Above all, the qualities of Teresa's intense love and devotion, and the ways that the life of prayer brings one into a closer, more loving and intimate relationship with God, burst forth from *The Way of Perfection*.

A Word About the Text

I have used E. Allison Peers' translation of *The Way of Perfection*. This translation appears in *St. Teresa's Complete Works: Volume II*, London: Sheed and Ward, 1946. Peers is the most respected of Teresa scholars, and I have benefited enormously from this translation, for Peers includes references to all the textual variants of the extant manuscripts of *The Way of Perfection*. Peers' use of both the major extant versions of Teresa's great work offers insight not only into her life and work as a writer but also into the elements of the writing style that so well characterizes Teresa's writing.

Since Teresa wrote this book for her nuns at the community at St. Joseph's in Avila, there are passages that refer specifically to explicit rules of their convent. I have thus eliminated two chapters— Chapter 3 and Chapter 5—that deal so directly with issues of living in a religious order that they are not broadly appealing. In addition, I have often deleted references to "my sisters" where Teresa is addressing her convent but where her words have a broad meaning and application. For the most part I have also deleted Teresa's references to Lutherans as heretics and ungodly people as well as her references to women as being particularly wicked and weak creatures incapable of reform.

Although I have deleted certain chapters, I have retained the original numbers of each chapter. Each chapter opens with a brief description of its contents.

I have remained true to the spirit of the text, even where I have mildly modernized it. Mostly, my modernizations have come in three areas. First, I have replaced archaic words and forms of address with more modern ones. Thus, "Thou," and its related pronoun forms, becomes "You," and its related forms, throughout. Second, I have attempted to use inclusive language in this edition, but I have retained the masculine pronouns for God so as not to be anachronistic. Finally, I have altered Teresa's syntax and sentence structure to make it livelier and more appealing to a contemporary audience. Most often this simply means casting sentences in the active rather than the passive voice.

I hope that Teresa's words will speak to you today even as they spoke to her sisters over 500 years ago.

Henry L. Carrigan, Jr.
Lancaster, Pennsylvania

BOOK CALLED
WAY OF PERFECTION

General Argument of this Book

This book discusses maxims and counsels that Teresa of Jesus gives to her daughters and sisters in religion, who belong to the Convents that, with the favor of Our Lord and the glorious Virgin, Mother of God, she has founded. She addresses the book especially to the sisters of the Convent of St. Joseph of Avila, the first Convent, where she was Prioress when she wrote this book.

Protestation

I submit all that I set in this book to the teachings of Our Mother, the Holy Roman Church. If there is anything in this book contrary to these teachings, I am unaware of it. For the love of Our Lord, I ask the scholars who revise the book to read it carefully and correct any faults of this kind and any others they may find. If there is anything good in this book, let this be to God's honor and glory and in the service of His most sacred Mother, our Patroness and Lady, whose habit I unworthily wear.

Prologue

Knowing that I have permission from my confessor Father Presentado Fray Domingo Banes to write certain things about prayer, the sisters of this Convent of St. Joseph have, out of their great love for me, earnestly appealed to me to say something to them about this subject. Since it seems that I will be successful in discussing this matter because of my acquaintance with many holy and spiritual persons, I have resolved to obey the sisters' wishes. I realize that their great love for me may render the imperfection and poverty of my style more acceptable than other books that are more ably written by those who know their subjects. I depend upon their prayers, by means of which the Lord might give me the insight and strength to say something concerning the way and method of life that this community should practice. If I do not succeed in doing this, Father Presentado, who will be the first to read what I have written, will either correct it or burn it. I shall have lost nothing by obeying my sisters, and they will see how useless I am when His Majesty does not help me.

I intend to suggest a few remedies for a number of small temptations that come from the devil which, because they are so slight, may pass unnoticed. I will also write about other things as the Lord reveals them to me and as they come to my mind. Since I don't know what I am going to say I can't set it down in a suitable order. I think it is better for me not to do so anyway, since it is quite unsuitable for me to be writing in this way at all. May the Lord lay His hand on all that I do so that it may be in accordance with His holy will. This is always my desire, although my actions may be as imperfect as I am.

I know I lack neither the love nor the desire to do all I can to help the souls of my sisters make great progress in the Lord's service. It may be that this love, combined with my years and my experience with a number of convents, will make me more successful than scholars in writing about small matters. I will not speak about anything I have not experienced myself, either in my own life or in observing others, or which the Lord has not taught me in prayer.

A few days ago I was commanded to write an account of my life in which I also discussed certain matters about prayer. My confessor may not wish you to see this writing, so I have set down in this book some of the things I said in that one as well as others that seem to me necessary. May the Lord direct this, as I have implored Him to do, and order it for His greater glory. Amen.

CHAPTER
I

When this convent was originally founded, I had not intended for there to be so much severity in external matters nor that there should be no regular income. Instead, I hoped that there would be no possibility of want. I acted, in short, like the weak and wretched woman I am, although I did so with good intentions and not out of consideration for my own comfort.

At about this same time, I noticed the harm and havoc that the Lutherans were wreaking in France and the way that their unhappy sect was growing. This development troubled me very much, and I wept before the Lord and begged Him to remedy this great evil. I would have laid down a thousand lives to save a single one of all the souls being lost there. Even though I am a woman and a sinner, incapable of doing all I would like to do in God's service, my whole desire is to do the little that is in me, especially since He has so many enemies and so few friends that His friends should be trusted ones. Therefore, I strove to follow the evangelical counsels as perfectly as I could and to see that these few nuns here should do the same, confiding in God's great goodness, for He never fails to help those who decide to forsake everything for His sake. As these nuns are all I have ever imagined them to be, I hoped that their virtues would more than counteract my defects, and I should be able to give the Lord some pleasure. By busying ourselves in prayer for those who are defenders of the Church, all of us would do everything we could to aid my Lord. He is so oppressed by those to whom He has shown so much good that it appears that these traitors would send Him to the Cross again and that He would have nowhere to lay His head.

Oh, my Redeemer, my heart cannot imagine this without being sorely distressed. What has become of Christians now? Must those who owe You the most always be those who distress You most? Those to whom You do the greatest kindnesses, whom You choose for Your friends, among whom You move, communicating Yourself to them through the Sacraments? Do they not think, Lord of my soul, that they have made You endure more than sufficient torments?

Certainly, my Lord, in these days withdrawal from the world means no sacrifice at all. Since worldly people have so little respect for You, what can we expect them to have for us? Can it be that we deserve that they should treat us any better than they have treated You? Have we done more for them than You have done that they should be friendly to us? What then? What can we expect, then, we who, because of God's goodness, are free from that pestilential infection and do not belong to the devil? They have won severe punishment at his hands, and their pleasures have richly earned them eternal fire. So to eternal fire they will have to go. Nonetheless, it breaks my heart to see so many souls traveling to perdition. I wish the evil were not so great and I did not see more being lost every day.

Oh, my sisters in Christ, help me to petition this of the Lord, Who has brought you together here for that very purpose. This is your calling; it must be your business; these must be your desires, your tears, your petitions. Let us not pray for worldly things, my sisters. It makes me laugh, yet makes me sad, when I hear of the things that people have come here to beg us to pray to God for. We are to ask the Lord for money and to provide them with incomes; I wish some of these people would petition God to enable them to trample all such things beneath their feet. Their intentions are quite good, and I do as they ask because I see they are really devout people. But I do not believe God ever hears me when I pray for such things. The world is on fire. People try to condemn Christ once again, for they bring a thousand false witnesses against Him. They would burn His Church to the ground, and we are to waste our time on things, that, if God were to grant, would bring one less soul to Heaven? No, my sisters, this is no time to pray for things of little importance.

If it weren't necessary to consider human frailty, which is satisfied with every kind of help, I would want it to be understood that God should not be entreated with such anxiousness for things like these.

My sisters, don't think that you will not have food just because you don't try to please everyone in the world. You won't go hungry, I assure you. Never use human trickery or deceit to get food or you will die of hunger, and rightly so. Keep your eyes fixed on your Spouse. He will sustain you. If He is pleased with you, even those who like you the least will give you food, as you have found by experience. If you should do as I say and still die of hunger, then happy are the nuns of St. Joseph's! For the love of the Lord, do not forget: You have given up a regular income; refrain from worries about food also, or you will lose everything. If the Lord wishes people to live on an income, let them do so, for it is their calling and they are justified. For us to do so, sisters, would be inconsistent.

Worrying about getting money from other people seems to me like thinking about what other people enjoy. No matter how much you worry, you will not make them change their minds nor will they suddenly want to give you money. Leave these anxieties to Him Who can move everyone, Who is the Lord of all money and all who possess money. It is by His command that we have come here and His words are true and cannot fail; Heaven and earth will fail first. Let us not fail Him, and let us have no fear that He will fail us. If He should ever do so it will be for our greater good, just as the saints failed to keep their lives when they were slain for the Lord's sake, and their happiness was increased through their martyrdom. We would be making a good trade if we could be finished quickly with this life and enjoy everlasting fullness.

Remember, sisters, that this will be important when I am dead; so, I am leaving it to you in writing. Since I know by experience what a great help it will be to you, I will remind you of it myself as long as I live. I have the fewest worries when I possess least, and the Lord knows that I am more afflicted when I have an excess of anything than when I have a lack of anything. I am not sure if it's the Lord's doing, but I have noticed that He provides for us immediately. To act in any other way would be to deceive the world by pretending to be poor when we are not poor in spirit but only poor outwardly. It seems to me this would be like stealing what is being given to us. Those who worry too much about the offerings they are likely to be given will one day find that such a bad habit will lead them to ask for something they do not need from someone who needs it more than they. Although that person would gain rather than lose by giving it to us, we would certainly be the worse off for having it. God forbid this should ever happen, my daughters. If it were likely to happen, I'd prefer you to have a regular income.

My daughters must believe that it is for their own good that the Lord has allowed me to experience in some small ways the blessings of holy poverty. Those who practice will also realize this, although not as clearly as I do. Even though I claimed to be poor, I was not poor in spirit, and my spirit lacked all restraint. Poverty is good and contains within itself all the good things in the world. Those who do care nothing for the good things of the world have dominion over all of them. What do kings and lords matter to me if I have no desire for their money, or to please them, if by doing so I displease God? What do their honors mean to me since I have realized that the primary honor of a poor person resides in his being truly poor?

I believe that honor and money nearly always go together. People who long for honor never hate money, while those who hate money do not care much about honor. I think this concern with honor always implies a consideration of money. A poor person is seldom honored by the world, no matter how worthy of honor he might be. The world will more likely despise this person than honor him. A different kind of honor, to which no one can object, comes with true poverty. If one embraces poverty solely for God's sake, only God has to be pleased. A person who does not need anyone has many friends; I have found this to be true from my own experience.

Our arms are holy poverty, which was so greatly honored and strictly observed by our holy Fathers at the beginning of our Order. Someone has said that they never kept anything from one day to the next. For the love of the Lord, then, let us strive to observe the rule of poverty inwardly since it is now less perfectly observed outwardly. Our life lasts just a few hours; our reward is boundless. Even if there were no reward but to follow the counsels God has given us, imitating His Majesty to any degree would bring us great compensation.

At all costs we must keep this rule of poverty as it applies to our community, our clothes, our speech, and, most important, our thoughts. As long as we do this, we don't need to worry that religious observances in our community will decline, for, as St. Clare said, the walls of poverty are very strong. It was with the walls of poverty and the walls of humility, she said, that she wanted to surround her convents. If the rule of poverty is truly kept, chastity and all other virtues are reinforced better than by any impressive and magnificent buildings. I wish that on the day you erect such buildings that they will fall down.

It seems very wrong, my daughters, that great houses should be built with poor people's money. May God forbid this. Let our houses be small and poor in every way. Let us be like our King, Who had no house except the porch in Bethlehem where he was born and the cross on which He died. These were houses where little comfort could be found. Those who build large houses no doubt have good reasons for doing so; they are moved by various holy intentions. But any corner is sufficient for thirteen poor women. Let there be a few hermitages where the sisters may go to pray. God preserve us from building a large ornate convent with a lot of buildings. Always remember that these things will fall down on the Day of Judgment, and who knows how soon that will be?

It would hardly look well if the house of thirteen poor women made a great noise when it fell, for those who are really poor must make no noise. Unless the truly poor live a noiseless life people will never take pity on them. My sisters will be very happy if they see someone freed from hell because of the offerings he has given them. This is possible since they are strictly bound to offer continual prayer for people who give them food. It is also God's will that, though the food comes from Him, we should thank the people by whose means He gives it to us. Do not neglect this.

May His Majesty always keep us in His hand so that we may never fall.

CHAPTER

4

Now, my daughters, you have seen the great task that we are trying to carry out. What kinds of people will we have to be if we do not want to be considered overly bold in God's eyes and in the world's eyes? It is clear that we need to work hard and it will help us greatly to have sublime thoughts so we may strive to make our actions sublime as well. If we strive carefully to observe our Rule and Constitutions in the fullest sense, I hope the Lord will grant our requests. I am not asking anything new of you, my daughters, only that we should practice faithfully our calling.

Our Rule tells us to pray without ceasing. Provided we perform this act as carefully as possible, we will not fail to observe the fasts, disciplines, and periods of silence commanded by the Order. These things must reinforce genuine prayer; prayer cannot be accompanied by self-indulgence.

You have asked me to say something to you about prayer. Before I speak about the interior life, that is, about prayer, I will speak of certain things which those walking along the way of prayer must practice.

These things are so necessary that even people who are not greatly interested in contemplation can advance a long way in the Lord's service. However, unless they have these things they cannot possibly be great contemplatives, and if they think they are, they are mistaken. May the Lord help me in this task and teach me what I need to say, so it may be to his glory.

Do not think, my friends and sisters, that I am going to instruct you to do many things. I hope the Lord will be pleased that we do those things that our holy Fathers ordained and practiced. There are only three things which I will explain at some length and which are taken from our Constitution. It is essential that we understand how important they are in helping us preserve our inward and outward peace. One of these is love for each other. The second is detachment from all created things. The third, true humility, is the most important of these and embraces all the rest.

Love for each other is of very great importance. Anything, no matter how annoying, can be easily borne by those who love each other. Anything which causes annoyance must be quite exceptional. If the world kept this commandment, I believe it would take us a long way toward keeping the rest. But, because we have either too much or too little love for each other, we never manage to keep it perfectly. It may seem that to have too much love for each other cannot be wrong, but I do not think anyone who had not witnessed it would believe how much evil and how many imperfections can result from this. The consciences of those who aim at pleasing God in provisional ways seldom observe the devil's snares. They think they are acting virtuously. However, those aiming at perfection understand these snares very well. Little by little the devil's snares deprive the will of the strength it needs to love God wholly.

One result of this is that all the nuns do not love each other equally. Some injury done to a friend is resented. A nun desires to have something to give to her friend or tries to make time for talking to her. Often her object is to tell her how fond she is of her, and other irrelevant things, rather than how much she loves God. These intimate friendships rarely focus on the love of God. I am more inclined to believe that the devil initiates them so as to create factions within religious Orders. When the object of a friendship is to serve God, it becomes clear that the will is empty of passion and is helping to conquer other passions.

In our community, we must all be friends with each other, love each other, be fond of each other, and help each other. For the love of the Lord, refrain from making individual friendships, however holy, for even among brothers and sisters such things are likely to be poisonous and I can see no advantage in them. Believe me, sisters, though I may seem extreme to you in saying so, great perfection and great peace come from following my advice, and those who are not very strong may avoid many occasions of sin. If our will leans more to one person than to another, we must exercise firm restraint on ourselves and not allow ourselves to be conquered by our affection. Let us love the virtues and inward goodness, and let us always apply ourselves and take care to avoid attaching importance to externals. Let us not allow ourselves, sisters, to be the slave of anyone except Christ.

We must be strictly on guard the moment that such a friendship begins, and we must proceed lovingly and diligently rather than severely. One effective precaution against this is that the sisters should not be together except at the prescribed hours. They should follow our present custom of not talking with one another or being alone together. Each one should be alone in her cell. It is easier to be silent if one is alone, and getting used to solitude is a great help to prayer. Since prayer must be the foundation on which this community is built, it is necessary for us to learn to like whatever helps us the most in our prayer.

Returning to the question of our love for one another, it seems quite unnecessary to commend this to you. For where are there people so brutish that they do not love one another when they live together, are continually in one another's company, indulge in no conversation, association, or recreation with anyone outside their house and believe that God loves them and that they love God since they are leaving everything to Christ? Virtue always attracts love, and I pray to God that there will always be love in the sisters of this community. It seems to me, therefore, that I do not need to commend this mutual love to you any more.

I would like, though, to say a little about the nature of this mutual love and how we will have this virtue. If you find this explained in great detail in other books, take no notice of what I am saying here, for it may be that I do not know what I am talking about.

There are two kinds of love that I am describing. The one is purely spiritual and apparently has nothing to do with sensuality or the tenderness of our nature. Either of these might stain its purity. The other is also spiritual, but it is mingled with our sensuality and weakness. Yet, it is a worthy love, much like the love between relatives and friends.

I want to speak about the first kind of spiritual love now. It is free from any sort of passion, for such a thing would completely spoil its harmony. If it leads us to treat virtuous people, especially confessors, moderately and discretely, it is profitable. If the confessor is at all vain, though, he should be regarded with suspicion. In such a case, conversation with him, no matter how edifying, should be avoided. The sister should make her confession briefly and say nothing more. It would be best for her to tell the superior that she does not get along with him and go somewhere else. This is the safest way.

Reflect on the great importance of this, for it is a dangerous matter and a source of harm to everyone. Do not wait until a great deal of harm has been done, but take every possible step to stop the trouble from the beginning. I hope the Lord will not allow people who are to spend their lives in prayer to have any attachment to anyone except one who is a great servant of God. Unless they see that he understands their language and likes to speak to them of God, they cannot possibly love him, for he is not like them. If he is such a person, he will have few opportunities of doing any harm, and he will disturb neither his own peace of mind nor that of God's servants.

I will repeat that the devil can do a great deal of harm here that may not be discovered for a long time. Thus the soul striving for perfection may be gradually ruined without knowing how. If a confessor gives the occasion for vanity because he himself is vain, he will tolerate vanity in others. May God deliver us from things of this kind. It would be enough to unsettle all the nuns if their consciences and their confessors should give them exactly opposite advice. If they must have only one confessor, they will not know what to do, nor how to pacify their minds, since the very person who should be calming them and helping them is the source of the harm. You must not be surprised if I attach a great deal of importance to this matter, for in some places there is a great deal of this kind of trouble.

CHAPTER
6

L et us now continue talking about the love which it is good for us to feel. I have described such love as purely spiritual. I am not sure what I am talking about, but it seems to me that there is no need to speak much about this kind of love, since so few, I'm afraid, possess it. If the Lord has given such love to any of you, praise Him fervently, for you must be a person of the greatest perfection. Perhaps what I say may help some, for if you see a virtue, you desire it and try to gain it and become attached to it.

God grant that I may be able to understand this and be able to describe it, for I am not sure I know when love is spiritual and when there is sensuality mingled with it. I am like one who hears a person speaking in the distance and cannot understand his words. It is just like that with me: Sometimes I cannot understand what I am saying, yet the Lord helps me to say it well. If at other times what I say does not make sense, it is only natural for me to go completely astray.

It seems to me that one loves very differently from others when one has learned the great difference between this world and the other one. This world is only a dream and the other is eternal. One who knows the difference between loving the Creator and loving the creature also knows the difference between purely spiritual love and spiritual love mingled with sensuality. Those who have devoted themselves to being taught by God in prayer also love very differently from those who lack such devotion.

You may think it is irrelevant for me to talk about this, and you may say you already know everything I will say. God grant this may be so. If you know it, you will see that I am telling the truth when I say that the person the Lord brings this far does indeed possess this love. Those whom God brings to this state are generous souls. They are not content with loving anything so miserable as these bodies, no matter how beautiful the bodies are nor how much grace they have. If the sight of the body gives them pleasure, they praise the Creator. But they do not have love for the body for more than a moment. If they did have such love, they would think they were loving something insubstantial and developing fondness for a shadow. They would be ashamed of themselves and would not have the courage to tell God they love Him without feeling very confused.

You will say that such people cannot love or repay affection they are shown by others. Indeed, they care very little for this affection. They may experience a natural and momentary pleasure at being loved. As soon as they return to their normal condition, though, they realize that such pleasure is foolish, except when the persons concerned can benefit their souls by instruction or prayer. Any other kind of affection wearies them, for they know it cannot help them and may even harm them. Nevertheless, they are grateful for such affection and repay it by commending to God the ones who love them. Since they can see nothing lovable in themselves, they suppose the love comes from God and think that others love them because God loves them. So, they ask Christ to repay them for this, thus feeling that they have no more responsibility. I think this desire for affection is sometimes sheer blindness, except when it concerns people who can lead us to do good so we may gain blessings in perfection.

I should add here that when we desire anyone's affection we always seek it because of some interest, profit, or pleasure of our own. Those who are perfect, though, have trampled all these things beneath their feet. They have so despised this world's pleasures, delights, and blessings that they could not love anything outside God or unless it has to do with God. What can they gain, then, from being loved themselves?

When they think about the matter this way, they laugh at themselves for being so anxious in the past about whether or not their affection was being returned. No matter how pure our affection might be, though, it is quite natural for us to wish it to be returned. But the return of affection is insubstantial, like straw, as light as air and easily carried away by the wind. For, however dearly we have been loved, what is left for us? Such people, except for the advantage affection might bring to their souls (because they realize that it is in our nature soon to tire of life without love) do not care whether or not they are loved. Do you think that such people will love no one and delight in no one except God? No; they will love others much more than they did, with a more genuine love, with greater passion and with a love that brings more gain. In brief, that is what love really is. Such souls are much fonder of giving than receiving, even in their relations with God. This holy affection deserves the name of love, although the name of love has been stolen from it by those other base affections.

Yet, what attracts them if they do not love the things they see? They do love what they see and they are greatly attracted by what they hear, but the things they see are everlasting. If they love anyone, they immediately look right beyond the body, fix their eyes on the soul and see what there is to be loved in that. If there is nothing, but they see any suggestion that if they dig deep they will find gold within this mine, they will think nothing of the work of digging. They are doing this because of their love. They will do anything for the good of that soul since they want their love to be lasting. They know quite well that this is impossible unless the loved one has certain good qualities and a great love for God. Even if that soul were to die for them and perform all the kind actions in its power, this would be impossible. Even if the soul had all the natural graces joined in one, their wills would not be strong enough to love it or to remain fixed upon it. They have experienced all this and recognize its truth. They see that they are not in unison with that soul and that their love for it cannot possibly last. Unless that soul keeps the law of God, their love will end with life. They know that unless it loves Him that they will go to different places.

Those into whose souls the Lord has already infused true wisdom do not value this love, which lasts only on earth, for more than it is worth. Those who take pleasure in worldly things, delights, honors, and riches will judge it of some value if their friend is rich and can afford to bring them worldly pleasures. Those who already hate all this will care little or nothing for such things. If they have any love for such a person, it will be a passion that he may love God so as to be loved by God. They know that no other kind of affection can last and that this kind will cost them dearly. For this reason they do all they possibly can for the good of their friend. They would lose a thousand lives to bring him a small blessing. Oh precious love, forever imitating the Captain of Love, Jesus, our Good!

CHAPTER

7

It is strange to see how much passion this love provokes. It costs many tears, penances, and prayers. The loving soul is careful to commend the object of its affection to all who it thinks may prevail with God and to ask them to intercede with Him for this object of affection. The loving soul's longing is constant, and it cannot be happy unless it sees that its loved one is making progress. If the latter seems to have advanced and then falls back, her friend seems to have no pleasure in life. She does not eat or sleep and is always afraid that the soul whom she loves so much may be lost, and that the two may be parted forever. She is not concerned about physical death, but she cannot bear to be attached to something that a puff of wind may suddenly carry away. This is love without any degree of self-interest. All that this soul wishes is to see the soul it loves enriched with blessings from Heaven. This is love that grows to be more like Christ's love for us. It deserves the name of love and is quite different from our petty and frivolous earthly affections.

These last affections are indeed a hell. It is needless

for us to bother ourselves by saying how evil they are, for the least of the evils they bring are terrible beyond belief. We do not need ever to take such things to our lips, or even think of them, or to remember that they exist anywhere in the world. Do not ever listen to anyone speaking of such affections, either seriously or humorously, and do not allow them to be mentioned or discussed in your presence. No good can come from our discussing these affections, and it might do us harm even to hear them mentioned. But it is different regarding the lawful affections we have for each other and for relatives and friends. Our whole desire is that they should not die. If their heads ache, our souls seem to ache too. If we see them in distress, we are unable to sit still and watch it.

This is not the case with spiritual affection. Although our weak natures will at first allow us to feel sympathy for our friends, our reason soon begins to ponder whether or not our friend's trials are good for her. We wonder if these trials are making her more virtuous and how she is bearing them. Then we will ask God to give her patience for enduring trials that lead her to virtue. If we see she is being patient, we are not worried. Indeed, we are joyous and relieved. Even if she could be given all the rewards and gain that suffering is capable of producing, we would still prefer suffering ourselves to seeing her suffer. However, we are not worried or upset.

I repeat that this love is just like the love that Jesus, the good Lover, bore for us. It brings us such immense benefits, for it makes us embrace every kind of suffering, so that others, without having to endure the suffering, may gain its advantage. The recipients of such friendship gain much. Their friends should realize, however, that this exclusive friendship must come to an end or that they must pray fervently to God that their friend may walk in the same way as themselves, as Saint Monica did with Him for Saint Augustine. Their heart does not allow them to be false. If they see their friend straying from the road, they will speak to her about it. They cannot allow themselves to do anything else. After this, if the loved one does not change her ways, they will not flatter her or hide anything from her. Either she will change her ways or their friendship is over. Otherwise, they would be unable to endure it, for it would mean continual war for both parties. A person may be indifferent to all other people in the world and not worry whether or not they are serving God, since the person she has to worry about is herself. She cannot feel this way about her friends. Nothing they do can be hidden from her. She sees the smallest fault in them. This is a very heavy cross for her to bear.

Happy are the souls that are loved by such as these. Happy the day on which they came to know them. O my Lord, will You grant me the favor of giving me many who have such love for me? Truly,

Lord, I would rather be loved by these than by all the kings of the world, for such friends use every means in their power to give us dominion over the whole world and to have all that is in the world subject to us. Love such persons as much as you like. There can be very few of them, but it is the Lord's will that their goodness should be known. When you are striving for perfection, you will be told that you don't need to know such people; it is enough for you to know God. But, to get to know God's friends is a very good way of getting to know Him. As God is my witness, it is because of such people that I am not in hell. I was always very fond of asking them to commend me to God, and I prevailed upon them to do so.

It is this kind of love that I would like us to have. It may not be perfect at first, but the Lord will make it increasingly perfect. At first it may be mingled with emotion, but, as a rule, this will do no harm. It is sometimes good and necessary for us to feel and show emotion in our love and to be distressed by some of our friends' trials and weaknesses, however trivial. For on one occasion a small matter might cause as much distress as a great trial might cause on another occasion. There are people whose nature is very much affected by small things. If you are not like this, do not neglect to have compassion on others. It may be that Our Lord wishes to spare us these sufferings and give us sufferings of another kind that will seem heavy to us, though to others they may seem light. In these matters, we must not judge others by ourselves nor think of ourselves at some time when the Lord has made us stronger than they. Let us think about what we were like at the times when we have been the weakest.

We must try hard to recall what we were like when we were weak and remember that, if we are no longer weak, it is not our doing. Otherwise, little by little, the devil could easily cool our charity toward our neighbors and make us think that what is really a failing on our part is perfection. In every respect we must be careful and alert, for the devil never sleeps. The nearer we are to perfection, the more careful we must be, since his temptations are then much more cunning. If we are not cautious, the harm is done before we realize it. We must always pray and watch, for there is no better way than prayer of revealing those hidden wiles of the devil and making him declare his presence.

It is a very good thing for us to take compassion on each other's needs. Get to know the things in others that you would be sorry to see and those about which you should sympathize with them. Always show your grief at any of their obvious faults. It is a good proof and test of our love if we can bear with such faults and not be shocked by them. Others, in their turn, will bear with your faults, which, if you include those of which you are not aware, must be much more numerous. Commend to God often any friend who is at fault and strive on your own part to practice with perfection the virtue that is opposite of her fault. Make determined efforts to do this so that you may teach by actions what your friends could never learn by words nor gain through suffering.

The habit of performing some conspicuously virtuous action through seeing it performed by another is one that easily takes root. This is good advice: Do not forget it. The love of someone who can bring gain to everyone by sacrificing her own gain is true and genuine. She will make a great advance in each of the virtues. This will be a much truer kind of friendship than one that uses every possible loving expression. Keep phrases like "My life!" "My love!" and "My darling!" for your Spouse, for you will be so often alone with Him that you will want to use them all. If you use them among yourselves, they will not move the Lord so much.

If you should be cross with one another because of some hasty word, you must at once correct the matter and pray earnestly. The same applies to the harboring of any grudge or to the desire to be the greatest. If this should happen to you, consider yourselves lost. Just reflect and realize that you have driven your Spouse from His home. He will have to go and seek another abode, since you are driving Him from His own house. Cry aloud to Christ and try to correct things.

CHAPTER
8

We must practice detachment, for if we perform it perfectly it includes everything else. If we do not concern ourselves with created things, but embrace the Creator alone, God will infuse the virtues into us in such a way that we will not have to wage war much longer. The Lord will defend us from the devils and the whole world. Do you think, daughters, that it is a small benefit to get for ourselves this blessing of giving ourselves entirely to Him and of keeping nothing for ourselves? Since all blessings are in Him, let us praise Him heartily for having brought us together here. I do not know why I am saying this, when all of you here are capable of teaching me. I confess that, in this important respect, I am not as perfect as I should like to be. I must say the same about all the virtues and about all I am dealing with here, for it is easier to write about such things than to practice them.

As far as exterior matters are concerned, you know how completely cut off we are from everything. Oh, sisters, for the love of God, try to recognize the great favor the Lord has bestowed on those of us He has brought here. Let each of you apply this to herself, since there are only twelve of us and God has been pleased for you to be one. I know many people who are better than I who would gladly take my place, yet the Lord has granted it to me who so poorly deserves it. Blessed be You, my God, and let the angels and all created things praise You, for I cannot repay this favor any better than I can repay any of the others You have given me. It was a wonderful thing to call me to be a nun. But, I have been so wicked, Lord, that You could not trust me. In a place where there were many good women living together, my wickedness might have gone unnoticed. Indeed, I did conceal it from you for many years. But, You brought me here, where there are so few of us that my wickedness is impossible not to notice. You remove occasions of sin from me so that I may walk more carefully. There is no excuse for me, then, O Lord, I confess it, and so I need Your mercy so You may forgive me.

What I earnestly beg of you is that anyone who knows she will be unable to follow our customs will say so before she enters our community. There are other convents where the Lord is also well served, and she should not stay here and disturb these few of us whom God has brought together for His service. In other convents nuns are free to have the pleasure of seeing their relatives. Here, if relatives are ever admitted, it is for their own pleasure. A nun who wishes to see her relatives in order to see herself must, unless they are spiritual people and do her soul some good, consider herself imperfect and realize she is neither detached or perfect. She will have no freedom of spirit or perfect peace. If she does not lose this desire, she is not intended for this house.

The best remedy is that she should not see her relatives again until she feels free in spirit and has gained this freedom from God through many prayers. When she considers such visits as crosses to bear, let her receive them, for then the visits will do the visitors good and do her no harm. However, if she is fond of the visitors, if their troubles distress her greatly, and if she delights in listening to their stories about the world, she may be sure that she will do herself harm and do the visitors no good.

If we religious only understood how much harm comes from having so much to do with our relatives, how we would shun them. I do not see what pleasure they can give us or how they can bring us any peace or tranquility. For we cannot take part in their pleasures, since it is not lawful for us to do so. Though we can certainly share their troubles, we can never help weeping for them, sometimes more than they do themselves. If they bring us any bodily comforts, we will pay for it in our spiritual lives and our poor souls. But, you are free from that here. You have everything in common, and none of you may accept any private gift. The community holds all the offerings given to us. You are under no obligation to entertain your relatives in return for what they give you. The Lord will provide for all of us in common.

I do not know how much of the world we really leave when we say we are leaving everything for God's sake if we do not withdraw ourselves from the chief worldly thing—our relatives. The matter has become so serious that some people think that religious must lack virtue if they are not fond of their relatives or see them very much.

In this house, daughters, we must commend our relatives to God, for that is only right. In all other matters, we must keep them out of our minds as much as we can. It is natural, after all, that our desires be attached to them more than to other people. My own relatives were very fond of me, and I was so fond of them that I would not let them forget me. But I have learned through experience that it is God's servants who have helped me in trouble. My relatives, except for my parents, have not helped me very much. Parents are different, for they very rarely fail to help their children. It is right that when they need our comfort we should not refuse them. If we find that doing so does not harm our main purpose, we can give them help and remain completely detached.

Believe me, sisters, if you serve God as you should, then you will find no better relatives than those servants of God that He sends to you. If you keep on doing as you are doing here, and realize that by doing otherwise you will be failing your true Friend and Spouse, you will soon gain this freedom. Then you will be able to trust those who love you for His sake alone more than all your relatives. They will not fail you. You will find parents, brothers, and sisters where you least expected to find them. These people help us and look for their reward only from God. Those who look for rewards from us soon grow tired of helping us when they see we are poor and can do nothing for them.

All the advice the saints give us about withdrawing from the world is good. Attachment to our relatives is the thing that sticks to us most closely and is hardest to get rid of. People are right, then, to withdraw from their own part of the country, if it helps them. For I do not think it helps us so much to leave a physical place as to embrace the good Jesus, Our Lord, with the soul. Just as we find everything in Him, so for His sake we forget everything. Until we have learned this truth, though, it helps us to keep apart from our relatives. Later on, the Lord might want us to see them again so that what used to give us pleasure may be a cross to us.

Once we have detached ourselves from the world and are cloistered here without any possessions, it must look as if we have done everything and there is nothing left with which we must contend. But, my sisters, do not feel secure and fall asleep, or you will be like the person who bolted all her doors for fear of thieves only to find that the thieves were already in the house. Unless we take great care and each of us renounces her self-will, many things will deprive us of that holy freedom of spirit which allows our souls to soar to their Maker unburdened by the earth's heavy weight.

If we keep the vanity of all things constantly in our thoughts, we will be able to withdraw our affections from trivial things and fix them on eternal things. This may seem poor advice but it will fortify the soul greatly. We must be very careful, for as soon as we begin to grow fond of small things we must withdraw our thoughts from them and turn our thoughts to God. He has granted us the great favor of providing that, in this house, most of it is done already. But we must become detached from ourselves. It is difficult to withdraw from ourselves and oppose ourselves, because we are very close to ourselves and love ourselves very dearly.

This is where true humility can enter. True humility and detachment from self always go together. You must embrace them, love them, and never be seen without them. Oh, how sovereign are these virtues—mistresses of all created things, empresses of the world, our deliverers from the devil's snares—that our Teacher, Christ, so dearly loved and Who was never without them. The one who possesses them can safely go out and fight all the united forces of hell and the whole world and its temptations. This person does not need to fear anyone, for hers is the kingdom of the Heavens. She does not care if she loses everything; her sole fear is that she may displease God, and she begs Him to nourish these virtues within her so she will not lose them through any fault of her own.

These virtues are hidden from the one who possesses them, even if she is told that she has them. She prizes them so much, though, that she is always trying to obtain them. She thus perfects them more and more in herself. Those who possess them soon make the fact clear to anybody with whom they have contact. How inappropriate it is for me to begin to praise humility and sacrifice when these virtues are so highly praised by the King of Glory, a praise exemplified in all the trials He suffered. You must work to possess these virtues, my daughters, if you are to leave the land of Egypt. For when you have attained these virtues, you will also attain the manna. All things will taste well to you, and no matter how much the world may dislike their savor, to you they will be sweet.

We must first rid ourselves immediately of our love for our bodies. Some of us pamper ourselves so much that doing so will be hard work. It is also amazing how concerned some of us are about having a healthy body. Some of us think, though, that we embraced the religious life for no other reason than to keep ourselves alive. In our community, there is very little chance for us to act on such a principle. We have come here to die for Christ, not to practice self-indulgence for Christ. The devil tells us that we need to be self-indulgent if we are to keep the Rule of Our Order. So many of us try to keep the Rule by looking after our health that we die without having kept it for a even a day.

It is really amusing to see how some people torture themselves for their excessive behavior, for the real weakness in their souls. Sometimes they perform penances without any reason. They perform them for a few days and then the devil puts it in to their heads that they have been doing themselves harm and makes them afraid of penances. After this they don't even do what the Order requires. They do not keep the smallest points in the Rule, such as silence, which is quite incapable of harming them. If we imagine we have a headache, we stay away from choir. One day we are absent because we had a headache some time ago. Another day we are absent because our head has just begun to ache again. We are absent the next three days in case it aches any more. Then we want to invent penances on our own, and we end up doing neither one thing nor the other. Sometimes there is very little wrong with us, but we think it should release us from all our obligations.

Oh, God help me! that nuns should be complaining so much. May He forgive me, but I am afraid such complaining has become quite a habit. A nun began complaining to me about her headaches and went on complaining for a long time. When I questioned her about her pain, I found she did not have a headache at all but that she was suffering from some pain in another part of her body.

These are things that might sometimes happen, and I write about them so you may be on guard against them. If the devil begins to frighten us about losing our health, we will never get anywhere. May the Lord give us light so that we may act rightly in everything.

These continual moanings about trivial illnesses seem to me a sign of imperfection. If you can bear something, do not talk about it. A serious illness will draw attention to itself. Remember, there are only a few of you. If one of you gets into this habit, she will worry all the rest, assuming you love each other and there is charity among you. On the other hand, if one of you is really ill, she should say so and take the necessary medicine. If you have put aside your self-love, you will so regret indulging yourselves in any way that you will be afraid of self-indulgence without a proper cause. When such a reason does exist, it would be much worse to say nothing about it than to allow yourselves unnecessary indulgence. It would also be wrong if others were not sorry for you.

I am quite sure that if there is prayer and charity among you that you will always be taken care of. Do not complain about the weaknesses and minor ailments that women suffer, for the devil sometimes makes you imagine them. They come and go; unless you get out of the habit of talking and complaining about minor illnesses, they will always bother you. Our body has one fault: The more you indulge it, the more things it discovers that it has to have. It is extraordinary how the body likes to be indulged. If there is any reasonable pretext for indulgence, no matter how unnecessary it is, the poor soul is taken in and prevented from making progress. Think about how many poor people must be ill and have no one to complain to. Poverty and self-indulgence make bad company. Surely we have not come here to indulge ourselves more than they. You are free from the great trials of the world. Learn to suffer a little for the love of God without telling everyone about it. When a woman has made an unhappy marriage she does not talk about it or complain, for she does not want her husband to know. She has to endure a great deal of misery and she has no one to whom she may talk. Can't we, then, keep secret between God and us some of the afflictions He sends us because of our sins? Even more so, for talking about them does not help to lessen them.

I am not referring to serious illnesses, though with these, too, I ask you to observe moderation and to have patience. I am thinking of those minor afflictions that you might have. When afflicted in such a way, you can go about your daily offices without worrying everybody else about them. When there is one person who talks continually about her minor illnesses, it often happens that some suffer on account of others and others will not believe her when she says she is ill, no matter how serious her sickness might be. Let us remember our holy Fathers, the hermits whose lives we strive to imitate. What sufferings, solitude, cold, and burning heat, and hunger and thirst they bore. Yet they had no one to complain to except God. Do you think they were made of iron? They were as frail as we are. Once we begin to subdue these miserable bodies of ours, they give us much less trouble. There will be plenty of people to see to what you really need. Do not think about yourselves except when you know it is necessary. Unless we resolve to endure illness and death once and for all, we will never accomplish anything.

Try not to fear illness and death and commit yourselves to God. What does it matter if we die? How many times have our bodies ridiculed us? Shouldn't we occasionally ridicule them? If we make this resolution day by day, by the grace of the Lord we will be able to control our body. To conquer such an enemy is a great achievement in the battle of life. May the Lord grant, as He is able, that we may do this. I am quite sure that everyone who enjoys such a victory, which I believe is a great one, will understand the advantages it brings. No one will regret endured trials in order to attain this tranquility and self-mastery.

CHAPTER
12

There are some other little things we need to talk about, though they will appear trivial. This seems to be a great task, for it involves battling against ourselves. But once we begin to work, God works in our souls and bestows such favors on them that the most we can do in this life does not seem like very much. We are doing everything we can by giving up our freedom for the love of God and entrusting it to one another. We are doing our best to serve God by putting up with so many trials—fasts, silence, service in choir—that no matter how much we want to indulge ourselves we can only do so occasionally. In all the convents I have seen, I am the only nun guilty of self-indulgence. Why, then, do we shy away from interior sacrifice when it is the means by which every other kind of sacrifice can be practiced with greater tranquility and ease and with greater reward? We can acquire such self-sacrifice by gradual progress and by never indulging our will and desire, even in small things, and succeed in subduing the body to the spirit.

This consists entirely in our ceasing to care about ourselves and our own pleasures, for the least that anyone who is beginning to serve the Lord can offer Him is her life. Once she has surrendered her will to Him, what does she have to fear? If she is a true religious and person of prayer and strives to enjoy Divine consolations, she must not turn away from the desire to die and suffer martyrdom for His sake. The life of a good religious, who wants to be among God's closest friends, is one long martyrdom. How do we know that our lives will be so short that they will end only one hour or one moment after we decide to commit our entire service to God? We must not measure ourselves by anything that comes to an end, least of all by life, since not a day of it is secure. Who, if she thought that each hour might be her last, would not spend it working for God?

It is perhaps a good thing to think this way, for by doing so we can learn to subdue our wills in everything. If you are very careful about your prayer, you will soon find yourselves gradually reaching the top of the mountain without knowing how you have done so. How harsh it sounds to say we must not take pleasure in anything. But, we must remember what consolations and delights come from this renunciation and how much we gain from it, even in this life. As you all practice such renunciation, you have done the principal part. Each of you encourages and helps the rest. Each of you must try to outstrip her sisters.

Be careful about your inner thoughts, especially if they have to do with rank. May God, by His Passion, keep us from dwelling upon such thoughts as: "But I am her senior"; "But I am older"; "But I have worked harder"; "But that other sister is being treated better than I am." If you have these thoughts, you must quickly stop them. If you allow yourselves to dwell on them, or introduce them into your conversation, they will spread like the plague and in religious houses they may give rise to great abuses. Pray fervently for God's help in this matter.

You may say that God grants consolations to people who are not completely detached from such concerns with rank and honor. In His infinite wisdom He sees that this will enable Him to lead them to leave everything. By "leaving everything," I do not mean entering the religious life, for there may be obstacles to this. The perfect soul can be detached and humble anywhere. This soul will find it harder to be detached in the world, though, for worldly trappings will be an obstacle to it. Questions of honor and property can arise within convents as well as outside them. The more these kinds of temptations are removed from us, the more we are to blame if we yield to them. Though people who yield may have spent many years in prayer or meditation—for perfect prayer eventually destroys all these attachments—they will never make great progress or come to enjoy the real fruit of prayer.

Ask yourselves if these worldly things mean anything to you. The reason you are here is so that you may detach yourselves from them. You do not gain greater honor by having them, and these attachments lose you advantages that might have gained you more honor. Thus, you get both dishonor and loss at the same time. Let each of you ask herself how humble she is, and she will see how far she has come. If she is really humble, I do not think the devil will tempt her to be concerned about rank. If a humble soul is tempted by the devil in this way, her humility will bring her more courage and greater gain. Such a temptation will cause her to examine her life. It will cause her to compare the services she has given to her Lord with what she still owes Him. This temptation will cause her to think over her sins, to remember where she deserves to be on account of her sins, and to recall how our Lord humiliated Himself to give us an example of humility. The soul receives such great gain that Satan will not dare to come back again lest he should get his head broken.

God deliver us from people who wish to serve Him yet who are overly concerned with their own honor. Reflect upon how little they gain from this. The very act of wishing for honor robs us of it, especially in matters of rank. There is no poison in the world that is so fatal to perfection. You wonder why I am concerned about what you think are trivial things. They are not trivial; in religious houses they spread like foam on water, and there is no small matter like ceremoniousness about honor and sensitivity to insult. Its root might be in some small slight, and the devil will then persuade someone else to consider it important. She will think that it is kind to tell you about the slight and ask you how you can allow yourself to be insulted. She will pray that God will give you patience and that you will offer patience to God. The devil is simply putting his deceit in the other person's mouth. Though you are quite ready to bear this slight, you are tempted to vanity because you have not resisted something else as perfectly as you should have.

Our human nature is so wretchedly weak that, even though we tell ourselves there is nothing to make a fuss about, we imagine we are being virtuous. We begin to feel sorry for ourselves, especially when we see that other people feel sorry for us, too. In this way the soul begins to lose the rewards it had gained. It becomes weaker and opens a door to the devil that he can enter with a temptation worse than the last. Even when you are prepared to suffer an insult, your sisters say you ought to be more sensitive about things. For the love of God, my sisters, do not let charity move you to show pity for others who have been the targets of these imagined insults, for such pity is like the kind that Job's wife and friends showed him.

CHAPTER
13

Anyone who wants to be perfect must shun such phrases as: "I had right on my side"; "They had no right to do this to me"; "The person who treated me like this was not right." May God deliver us from such a false idea of right. Do you think it was right that our good Jesus had to endure so many insults? Were those who hurled insults at Him right, and did they have the right to do those wrongs to Him? I do not know why anyone is in a convent if she is willing to bear only those crosses she thinks she has a right to expect. She should return to the world. Do you think you can ever have to bear so much that you shouldn't have to bear any more? How does right enter in this matter?

Before we complain about not having our rights, let us first receive some honor or gratification, for it is certainly not right that we should have such kind treatment in this life. On the other hand, when someone mistreats us, I do not see why we complain. Either we are brides of this great King or we are not. If we are, what honorable wife does not accept her share of any dishonor done to her spouse, even though she may resist doing so? It is ridiculous to want to share in the kingdom of our Spouse Jesus Christ and not be willing to have any part in his dishonors and trials.

God keep us from being like that. Let the sister who thinks she is the least among others consider herself the happiest and most fortunate. If she lives her life as she should, she will, as a rule, lack no honor either in this life or in the next. Let us, my daughters, imitate the great humility of the most sacred Virgin, whose habit we wear and whose nuns we are ashamed to call ourselves. Let us imitate this humility in some degree, because no matter how much we humble ourselves, we fall short of being the daughters of such a Mother and the brides of such a Spouse. Try to refrain from the habits I have described, for what appears trivial today may be a venial sin tomorrow. Such a tendency is so infectious that if you leave it alone, the sin will not be the only one for very long.

We who live in a community should consider this carefully, so that we do not harm those who work to benefit us and set for us a good example. If we realize the great harm that is done by the bad habit of pomposity about our honor, we should rather die a thousand deaths than be the cause of such a thing. Only the body would die, whereas the loss of a soul is a great and endless loss. Some of us will die, but others will take our places. They might be more harmed by this one bad habit we started than they are benefited by many virtues. For the devil does not allow a single bad habit to disappear, and the weakness of our mortal nature destroys the virtue in us.

If any nun sees that she cannot endure and conform to the customs of this house, she would perform a great service to God if she would go away and leave the other sisters in peace. If it follows my advice, no convent will take her in until they have given her many years' probation to see if she improves. I am not talking so much about shortcomings affecting penances and fasts, for they are not so harmful. I am thinking of nuns who are of such a temperament that they like to be greatly honored and celebrated and who see others' faults but never recognize their own. The true source of such behavior is lack of humility. If God does not help this person by bestowing great spirituality upon her so that after many years she becomes greatly improved, may He preserve you from keeping her in your convent. You must realize that neither she nor you will have any peace there.

In this house you have risked losing worldly honor and forgone it. Do not desire that others should be honored at a cost to you. Our honor, sisters, lies in God's service. If anyone hinders you in this service, she should keep her honor and stay at home. A humble nun will not mind if she is not professed. She knows that if she is good she will not be sent away. If she is not, why should she wish to harm one of Christ's communities?

By not being good, I am referring to a lack of sacrifice and an attachment to worldly things and to self-interest. Let anyone who knows that she is not capable of great sacrifice not become a nun, if she does not want to suffer a hell on earth. God grant that there is not another hell waiting for such a nun in the next world.

The whole manner of life we are trying to live leads us to detach ourselves from all created things. I have observed that anyone the Lord has chosen for this life is granted that favor. She may not have it in full perfection, but her great joy and gladness in such detachment makes God's favor evident. She will never have anything to do with worldly things, for her delight will come from all the practices of the religious life. I say once more that anyone who is inclined to worldly things should leave the convent if she sees she is not making any progress. If she still wishes to be a nun, she should go to another convent.

This house is another Heaven, if it is possible to have Heaven on earth. Anyone whose sole pleasure lies in pleasing God and who does not care for her own pleasure will find our life a very good one. If she wants anything more, she will lose everything, for there is nothing more that she can have. A discontented soul is like a person suffering from severe nausea. She rejects all food, no matter how appetizing it is. Food that healthy persons eat only causes her greater nausea. Such a person will save her soul better in another convent. Although we allow time to attain complete detachment and inward sacrifice, outward detachment and sacrifice have to be practiced immediately so that no harm may come to the other nuns. Anyone who sees this being done, spends all her time in such good company, and at the end of six months or a year has made no progress will not make any progress even after many years. I do not say that such a nun must be as perfect as the rest, but she must be certain that her soul is gradually growing healthier.

I am sure that the Lord helps anyone who makes good resolutions to live in His service. For that reason we must look into the intentions of anyone who enters the religious life. She must not come simply to further her own interests, although even the Lord can perfect this intention if she is an intelligent person. If she is not intelligent, a person like this should not be admitted. She will not understand her own reasons for coming nor will she understand subsequent attempts to improve her. In general, a person who has this fault always thinks she knows better than the wisest person what is good for her. I believe this evil is incurable, since it is often accompanied by malice.

When an intelligent person begins to grow fond of what is good, she clings to it ardently, for she sees that it is the best thing for her. Although this may not bring her great spirituality, it will help her give beneficial advice and to make herself useful in many ways without troubling anybody else. I do not see how a person lacking intelligence can be useful in community life; she may even do a great deal of harm. This defect may not be obvious immediately. Many people talk well but have little understanding, while others do not speak so well, but they are intelligent and perform a great deal of good. There are also simple, holy people who are unskilled in business matters but who are very skilled at talking to God. You must ask many questions, then, before novices are admitted, and the probation period before admission should be very long.

This is something that everyone considers for herself, and she must pray to God about it. I implore God to give you light on this matter. Do not accept dowries, for if you accept them you might be in the position of having to keep a sister whose ways are not suitable to your house. You must not receive dowries from anyone, for to do so would be to harm the very person whom you hope to profit.

CHAPTER
15

I am writing in such a choppy fashion. I am just like a person who does not know what she is doing. Read it as best you can, for am I writing it as best as I can. Burn it if it is too bad. I really need leisure, and I have so little time for writing that sometimes a week passes and I have not written anything. So, I forget what I have said and what I wanted to say next. Now, making excuses for myself is very bad for me. I implore you not to copy me, for to suffer without making excuses is a rewarding and edifying habit of great perfection. Although I often teach this to you, and by God's goodness you practice it, God has never granted this favor to me. I hope He will be pleased to grant it to me before I die.

I am greatly confused about urging this virtue upon you, for I ought to have practiced a little bit of what I am recommending to you. I confess, though, that I have made very little progress. I always seem to be able to find a reason for thinking I am being virtuous when I make excuses for myself. There are times when this might be lawful, and when not to do it would be wrong, but I don't have the discretion or humility to do it only when it is appropriate. It takes great humility to remain silent when you find yourself unjustly condemned. To do so would be to imitate our Lord Who sets us free from all our sins. Try earnestly to act this way, for it brings great gain. I can see no gain in trying to free ourselves from blame except in those very few cases where hiding the truth might be offensive or cause a scandal.

It is very important to practice this virtue and strive to obtain from the Lord the true humility that comes from this virtue. The truly humble person will have a genuine desire to be thought little of, persecuted and condemned unjustly. If she wants to imitate the Lord, how can she do better than this? No bodily strength is necessary here, only God's help.

These are great virtues, my sisters, and I would like for us to study them closely and to make them our penance. I deplore all excessive penances that, if practiced without discretion, injure our health. Here, though, there is no reason to be afraid. No matter how great the interior virtues are, they do not weaken the body so that it cannot serve the Order. These virtues strengthen the soul, can be applied to very little things, and they prepare one to gain great victories in very important matters.

It helps us greatly to meditate on the gains that such virtue brings us. No one can ever blame us unjustly, since we are always full of faults, and a just person falls seven times a day. It would be a falsehood to say that we have no sin. Even if we are not guilty of the thing we're accused of, then, we are never entirely without blame in the way that our good Jesus was.

Oh, my Lord! When I think of the many ways You suffered, many of them undeservedly, I do not know what to say for myself. I don't know what I must have been thinking when I wished for no suffering or what I am doing when I make excuses for myself. For what is it to You, Lord, to give much rather than little? I do not deserve it, but I have not deserved the favors You have already shown me. How can it be that I should want others to think well of someone so evil as me, when they have said such wicked things about You, Who are good above all other good? It is intolerable, my God. I do not want You to have to tolerate in me anything that is displeasing in your eyes. Give me light and make me want fervently that all should hate me, since I have often left You, Who have loved me so faithfully.

What advantage do we hope to gain from giving pleasure to creatures? What does it matter to us if they all blame us, if we are without blame in the Lord's sight? Oh, my sisters, we will neither succeed in understanding this truth nor in perfection unless we meditate upon what is real and what is not. There is a great gain in the confusion felt by your accuser when she sees that you allow yourselves to be condemned unjustly. Such an experience lifts up the soul more than ten sermons. We must all try to be preachers by our deeds, since both the Apostle

Paul and our own lack of ability forbid us to be preachers in word.

Do not suppose that either the evil or the good you do will remain secret, no matter how strictly you are enclosed. Do you think, daughters, that, if you do not make excuses for yourself, there will not be someone else who will defend you? Remember how the Lord took the Magdalene's part in the Pharisee's house and also when her sister blamed her. He will not treat you as rigorously as He treated Himself. It was not until He was on the Cross that He had even a thief to defend Him. Our Lord will put it into someone's mind to defend you; if He does not, it will be because there is no need. Be glad when you are blamed, and in time you will see what gains your soul experiences. In this way you will begin to gain freedom. Soon you will not care whether they speak ill or well of you. It will seem like someone else's business. It will be as if two people are talking in your presence and you are uninterested in what they are saying because they are not addressing you. This may seem impossible to those of us who are very sensitive and incapable of great sacrifice. Although it is very difficult at first, it is quite possible, with the Lord's help, to attain gradually this freedom, renunciation, and self-detachment.

CHAPTER
16

You have asked me to tell you about the first steps in prayer. Although God did not lead me by these steps, I know of no others, and even now I can hardly have acquired these elementary virtues. Anyone who does not know how to set out the pieces in a chess game will never be able to play well. If she does not know how to give check, she will not be able to bring about a checkmate. You will probably criticize me for using the example of games, since we do not play them in this house and are forbidden to do so. That will show you what kind of mother God has given you; she even knows about such vanities. However, they say that the game is sometime legitimate. If we play it frequently, we will give check to this Divine King. He will not be able to move out of our check nor will He want to do so.

The queen gives the king the most trouble in this game, and all the other pieces support her. No queen can beat this King as well as humility can. Humility brought Him down from Heaven into the Virgin's womb, and with humility we can draw Him into our souls by a single hair. You can be sure that He will give the most humility to the one who already has the most and the least to the one who has the least. Humility cannot exist without love, and love cannot exist without humility. It is impossible for these virtues to exist except where there is great detachment from all created things.

My daughters, you wonder why I am talking to you about virtues when you have more than enough books to teach you about them and when you want to know only about contemplation. If you had asked me about meditation, I could have talked to you about it and advised you to practice it, even if you have none of the virtues. This is the first step to take in acquiring the virtues. The life of all Christians depends on their beginning it. No one, no matter how lost a soul she is, should neglect so great a blessing if God inspires her to use it. I have written about all of this already, and so have many others who know what they are about.

Contemplation is another matter. This is an error that we all make. If someone spends a short time each day thinking about her sins, as she is bound to if she is more than a nominal Christian, people immediately call her a great contemplative. They expect her to have the rare virtues that a great contemplative is bound to possess. She may even think she possesses them, but she is wrong. In her early stages, she did not even know how to set up the chessboard. She even thought that simply recognizing the game pieces would be enough to enable her to give checkmate. This is impossible, though, for this King does not allow Himself to be taken except by one who surrenders entirely to Him.

If you want me, then, to talk about contemplation, allow me to talk a while about such matters, even if they seem trivial to you. If you do not want to hear about them or practice them, continue your mental prayer. But I can assure you that you will not acquire true contemplation. I may be wrong about this, of course, but I have been striving after contemplation for twenty years and still do not possess it.

I will now explain what I mean by mental prayer. God grant that we may practice it as we should. Although the virtues are not as necessary to mental prayer as to contemplation, we will have to work very hard to achieve mental prayer if we do not have the virtues. The King of glory will not come to be united with our souls unless we strive to gain the greatest virtues. God is sometimes pleased to show great favor to persons who are in an evil state and raise them to perfect contemplation. By this means He may snatch them out of the devil's hands. They may be in an evil state, yet the Lord will allow them to see a vision in order to draw them back to Him. I cannot believe, though, that He would grant them contemplation. For contemplation is a Divine union, where the Lord delights in the soul and the soul delights in the Lord. There is no way that the Purity of the Heavens can take pleasure in an unclean soul. The angels' Delight cannot be delighted in that which is not His own. We know that a soul becomes the property of the devil when it commits a mortal sin. Thus the soul takes its delight in the devil, since it has given him pleasure. The devil's delights, even in this life, are continual torture. My Lord will have no lack of children of His own in whom He may rejoice without going and taking others' children. Yet, God will do what He often does and snatch them out of the devil's hands.

Oh, my Lord, how often we make You wrestle with the devil. Wasn't it enough that You taught us how to conquer him when You allowed him to carry You in his arms when he took you to the Temple's pinnacle? What a sight it must have been, my daughters, to see this Sun by the side of the darkness. What fear that wretched creature must have felt, without knowing why, for God did not allow Him to understand. We should be grateful for such mercy and pity. We Christians ought to feel great shame at making Him wrestle every day with such an unclean beast. Your arms were certainly strong, my Lord, but why weren't they weakened by the trials and tortures You endured on the Cross? How quickly everything borne for love's sake heals again. If You had lived longer, the love You have for us would have healed Your wounds again and You would have needed no other medicine. Who will give me such medicine for all my trials? I would eagerly embrace all my sufferings and trials if I knew that I could be cured by such a health-giving ointment.

There are souls God knows He may gain for Himself by this means. Seeing that they are completely lost, God wants to leave no stone unturned to help them. Even though they lack virtues, He consoles them so that they begin to desire Him. He even occasionally brings them to a state of contemplation, though rarely and usually for a short time. He is testing them to see whether His grace will encourage them to prepare themselves to enjoy it often. If it does not, forgive them. Forgive us, O Lord, for it is dreadful that a soul You have brought near to You should become attached to worldly things.

I believe there are many souls that God tests in this way. There are few, though, who prepare themselves to enjoy God's grace. When the Lord does this and we leave nothing undone either, He never ceases from giving until He has brought us to a high degree of prayer. If we do not give ourselves to Him as He does to us, He will be doing more than enough for us if He leaves us in mental prayer, visiting us from time to time as He would visit servants in His vineyard. But these others are His beloved children whom He would never want to banish from His side. Since they have no desire to leave Him, He never does so. He seats them at His table and feeds them with His own food, almost taking the food from His mouth in order to give it to them.

We will be happy if we can leave these few and

petty things and arrive at a higher estate. Even if the whole world blames you, what does it matter as long as you are in God's arms? He is powerful enough to free you from everything; only once did He command the world to be made and it was done. With Him, to will is to do. Do not be afraid if He takes pleasure in speaking to you. He does this for the greater good of those who love Him. His love for those who hold Him dear is not weak; He shows us in every possible way. Why, then, do we not show Him our highest love? Think about how wonderful it is if we give Him our love and receive His. He can do all things, and we can do nothing here below except what He enables us to do. What do we do for You, O Lord, our Maker? We hardly do anything. If God is pleased that we should win everything by doing a mere nothing, let us not be so foolish as to fail to do it.

O Lord, all our troubles come to us because we do not have our eyes fixed on You. If only we looked at the path we're walking, we would soon arrive. But, we stumble and fall a thousand times and we stray because we do not set our eyes on the true Way. It seems so new to us that one would think no one before us had ever walked this way. It hardly seems that we are Christians at all or that we have ever in our lives read about the Passion. Lord help us that we should be hurt about some small point of honor. We refuse to be hindered by the smallest matter of rank. We cry out at once: "Well, I'm no saint."

God deliver us from saying, "We are not angels," or "We are not saints," whenever we commit some sin. We may not be. But, what a good thing it is for us to reflect that we can be if we will only try and if God gives us His hand. Do not be afraid that He will fail to do His part if we do not fail to do ours. Do not let there be anything we know of which would serve the Lord and which, with His help, we would not do. We must always have courage, which God gives to the strong. He will give courage to you and to me.

I have strayed far from the point. I want to return to explain the nature of mental prayer and contemplation. It may seem irrelevant, but it is all done for your sakes. You may understand it better as I express it in my rough style than in other books that put it more elegantly. May the Lord grant me His favor, so that this may be so.

Even though I am beginning to talk about prayer, I still have a little more to say about humility. Humility is the principal virtue that people who pray must practice. It is important that you should try to learn how to practice it often. How can anyone who is truly humble think she is as good as those who become contemplatives? Of course, in his goodness and mercy God can make her a contemplative. But my advice is that she should always sit in the lowest place, for that is what the Lord taught us to do by both His words and deeds. Let her prepare herself to let God lead her down this road if He so wills it. If not, she should consider herself happy in serving God's servants and in praising Him. Although she deserves to be a devil in hell, God has brought her here to live among His servants.

God does not lead us all by the same road, and maybe she who believes that she is going by the lowest road is the highest in God's eyes. Thus, it does not follow that just because we all practice prayer that we are all going to become contemplatives.

Those of us who are not contemplatives would be greatly discouraged if we did not understand the truth that contemplation is something given by God. Since it is not necessary for our salvation, God does not give it to us before He gives us our reward. We will not fail to attain perfection if we do these things. We may even acquire more merit, because what we do will require more work. The Lord will be laying up for us all that we cannot enjoy in this life. We should not be discouraged, then, and give up prayer or stop doing what the others are doing. The Lord might give us great rewards all at once as He has been giving to others over many years.

I myself spent over fourteen years without ever being able to meditate except while reading. There must be many people like this, and others who cannot meditate even after reading. They can only recite vocal prayers and they take a certain pleasure in being able to do this. Some find their thoughts wandering so much that they cannot concentrate upon the same thing. They are always restless. If they try to fix their thoughts on God, they are struck with a thousand foolish ideas and doubts concerning the Faith. I know a very old woman, a great servant of God, who has spent many years in vocal prayer but who is unable to get any help from mental prayer. The most she can do is to dwell upon each of her vocal prayers as she says them. There are a great many other people like this, and if they are humble, they will be very much like those who benefit from much encouragement. In one way they may feel safer, for we do not know whether encouragement comes from God or the devil. If it does not come from God, it is more dangerous. The chief object of the devil's work on earth is to fill us with pride. If encouragement comes from God, we need not be afraid. God's encouragement brings humility with it.

Others walk in humility and believe that it's their fault if they fail to receive encouragement. They are always anxious to make progress. They never see a person crying without thinking that they are not progressing in God's service unless they are also crying, even though they may be more advanced. For tears are not invariably signs of perfection. It is better to practice humility, sacrifice, detachment, and the other virtues. There is no reason for fear, and you must not fear that you will fail to attain the perfection of the greatest contemplatives.

Saint Martha was holy, but we are not told that she was a contemplative. What more could you want than to grow to be like her, who was worthy to receive Christ our Lord so often in her house, and to prepare meals for Him, and to serve Him and perhaps eat at table with Him? If she had been always absorbed in devotion, as Mary Magdalene was, no one would have prepared a meal for this Divine Guest. Remember that our little community is Saint Martha's house and that there are people of all kinds here. Nuns who are called to the active life must not murmur at others who are absorbed in contemplation. Contemplatives know that, although they themselves may be silent, the Lord will speak for them. As a rule, this makes them forget themselves and everything else.

Remember that there must be someone to cook the meals. Count yourselves happy in being able to serve like Martha. Remember that true humility consists in being ready for what the Lord wants to do with you and happy that He should do it, and in considering yourselves unworthy to be called His servants. If contemplation, mental and vocal prayer, tending the sick, serving in the house, and working at even the lowliest tasks serve the Guest who comes to stay with us, eat with us, and take His recreation with us, what should it matter if we do one of these things rather than another?

I do not mean that it is up to us to say what we will do. We must do our best in everything, for the choice is not ours but the Lord's. If after many years He is pleased to give each of us her office, it will be a curious kind of humility for you to wish to choose. Let the Lord do that, for He is wise and powerful and knows what suits you and Himself best. If God does not grant you contemplation, even though you have done everything in your power to prepare for high contemplation with the perfection I have already mentioned, it is because He has saved this joy to give to you in Heaven. He is pleased to treat you like a strong person and give you a cross to bear on earth like the one that Christ always carried.

What better sign of friendship is there than for Him to give you what He gave Himself? It might well be that you would not have had so great a reward from contemplation. His judgments are His own; we must not interfere with them. It is indeed a good thing that the choice is not ours. If it were, we would think contemplation a restful life and all become great contemplatives. We have a great deal to gain if we have no desire to gain what seems to us the best. Do not be afraid of losing God's encouragement. God never permits a truly sacrificial person to lose anything except when such a loss will bring her greater gain.

CHAPTER
18

I tell those of you whom God is not leading by the road of contemplation that, from what I have seen and heard, the contemplatives are not carrying a lighter burden than you. You would be amazed at the ways that God burdens them with their own crosses. I know about both types of life and I am well aware that the trials God gives to contemplatives are unbearable. If God did not encourage these contemplatives, they could not bear these trials. Since God leads those He loves the most by way of trials, it is clear that the more He loves them, the greater their trials will be. He does not hate contemplatives. With His own voice He praises them and calls them friends.

God would not acknowledge pleasure-loving people who are free from trials as His close friends. God gives these people great trials, and He leads them by such hard roads that they sometimes think that they are lost and will have to go back and begin again. Our Lord sustains them with wine so they may become drunk and not realize what they are going through and what they are capable of bearing.

I find few true contemplatives who do not suffer trials courageously and earnestly. If they are weak, the first thing the Lord gives them is courage so that they will not be afraid of any trials that may come to them.

When those who lead an active life sometimes see contemplatives receiving God's encouragement, they think that contemplatives experience nothing else. I can assure you that you might not be able to endure their sufferings for as long as a day. The Lord knows everyone as she really is and gives each one her work to do, according to what He sees to be most appropriate for her soul, for His own Self, and for her neighbor's good. Unless you are not prepared to do your work, you do not need to be afraid that your work will be done for nothing. We must all strive to do this. We are here for no other reason, and we must strive not merely for one year or ten, or it will look like we are giving up our work like cowards. The Lord should see that we are not leaving any work unfinished. We are like soldiers who, no matter how long they have served, must always be ready for their captain to send them away to perform any task he commands, since he is paying them. The Lord's payment is far richer than any payment made by this world's people.

When their captain sees they are all present, he assigns duties to them according to their fitness. If they were not present, our Heavenly Captain would not give them pay or service orders. Thus, practice mental prayers, sisters. If any of you cannot do that, practice vocal prayers, reading, and dialogue with God. Do not neglect the hours of prayer that all the nuns observe. You never know when the Spouse will call you and if He will give you fresh trials disguised as blessings. If He does not give you such trials, you may be sure that you are not fit for them and that your work suits you. True humility occurs when you think you are not fit for the work you are doing.

Perform cheerfully whatever work you are ordered to do. If such a worker is truly humble, she will be blessed in her active life and she will only complain of her failings. I would much rather be like her than some contemplatives. Let others fight their own battles, which are not easy ones. The standard-bearer does not fight, but he is exposed to great danger. Inwardly, he must suffer more than anyone, for he cannot defend himself, since he is carrying the flag and he cannot let go of it, even if he is killed. In the same way, contemplatives have to bear aloft the standard of humility and must suffer all the blows aimed at them without defending themselves. Their duty is to suffer as Christ suffered. They are given an honorable duty. The contemplative must reflect on her work. If she lets the standard fall, the battle will be lost. Those who are not so far advanced are greatly harmed when the captains and friends of God act in ways that are not appropriate to their office.

The other soldiers do the best they can. They will sometimes withdraw from extreme danger, but they do not lose honor because no one sees them. But, everyone looks at the actions of the captains and the friends of God. Their office is a noble one, and the King confers great honor and favor to whomever He gives it. Those who receive such offices do not accept a light obligation. Since we do not understand ourselves and do not know what we ask, we need to leave everything to God. He knows us better than we know ourselves. True humility consists in our being satisfied with what God gives us. There are some people who think that God owes them favors. Such humility is petty. The God Who knows us all does well in seldom giving things to such people. He sees clearly that they are unable to drink of His cup.

You may be certain that you have made progress, sisters, if each of you thinks she is the worst of all and shows that she thinks this by acting for the good of the rest. Progress does not mean enjoying the greatest amount of encouragement in prayer nor experiencing the greatest number of raptures or visions from God. We cannot know the value of those things until we reach the next world. Let us practice the great virtues of humility, sacrifice, and an obedience so strict that we never go an inch beyond the superior's orders. We know that her orders come from God since she is in His place. Obedience is the most important duty. Anyone who is disobedient is not a nun at all. But I will say no more since I am speaking to nuns I believe are good or at least want to be so.

If anyone under the vow of obedience goes astray by not observing the vow with a high degree of perfection, I wonder why she is in the convent. I can assure her that if she fails in this respect, she will never succeed in leading either a contemplative or an active life. Even someone who wants to achieve contemplation, but has not taken a vow of obedience, must be willing to surrender her will to a confessor who is a contemplative and will understand her. By doing this, she will make more progress in one year than in a great many years if she acts otherwise.

These are the virtues I want you to possess and strive to obtain. Do not be troubled because you do not have experience of those other kinds of devotion. It may be to some people that these kinds of devotion come from God. If they came to you, though, it might be because our Lord had permitted the devil to deceive you. Why do you want to serve the Lord in these doubtful ways when there are so many other legitimate ways of serving Him? Our nature is weak, but God will give strength to those to whom He offers contemplation. I am glad I have given this advice, for it will also teach contemplatives humility. If you say you do not need this advice, sisters, some of you might find this pleasant reading.

May the Lord give us light to follow His will in all things and we will have no reason to be afraid.

CHAPTER

19

Since I have not worked on this book for several days, I have forgotten much of what I was saying to you. However, I won't dwell on those matters much, and I won't worry too much about making connections in this chapter to things I've already written. If you have an orderly mind and are able to practice prayer in great solitude, you will benefit a great deal from the many books on prayer that have already been written by people more competent than I. There are books that describe the mysteries and the Passion of the Lord in short passages, one for each day of the week. There are meditations on the Judgment, on hell, on our own nothingness, and all we owe to God. These books contain helpful teachings as well as excellent methods for using well your time of prayer. If anyone already has the habit of practicing prayer in this way, the Lord will lead her to the harbor of light. If she begins well, she will also end well. Everyone who walks along this road will walk restfully and securely, for one always walks restfully when she restrains her understanding.

Some souls, though, are like wild horses that have not been broken. No one can stop them, for they wander constantly and are never still. A skilled rider may sometimes face danger when riding a horse like this. Even if the rider is unconcerned about death, there is always the risk that he will stumble, so he has to ride with great care. Some people are either like this by nature or God permits them to become like this. I am very sorry for them. They are like very thirsty people who see water a long way off. When they try to go to the water, they find someone who always prevents their reaching it, either at the beginning, the middle, or end of their journey. When they have defeated the first of these enemies after much strenuous work, they allow themselves to be defeated by the second. They prefer to die of thirst rather than drink water that is going to cost them so much trouble. Their strength has faded, and their courage has failed them. Some of these people are strong enough to defeat both the first and second enemies they meet. But, their strength fails when they meet the third enemy, even though they might be just a few steps away from the fountain of living water that the Lord promised would quench the thirst of whoever drank it. How right and true are the words that come from the lips of Truth Himself. The soul will never thirst for anything more in this life. Its thirst for things in the life to come will surpass any natural thirst we can imagine on this earth. How the soul longs to experience this kind of thirst. The soul knows how precious it is, for it creates the very satisfaction by which this thirst is quenched. It is a thirst that quenches nothing but the desire for earthly things. God satisfies it in such a way that one of the greatest favors He can bestow on a soul is to leave it with the desire to have a drink of this water again.

Water has three relevant properties that I can remember. One of them is its ability for cooling things. No matter how hot we are, water tempers the heat, and it will even put out a large fire.

Like those who drink this water now, sisters, you will be happy if God allows you to drink of it. You will understand how a genuine love of God, if it is strong and free from all earthly things, is master of all the elements and of the whole world. Since water comes from the earth, there is no fear that it will quench the fire of the love of God. Though the two elements are opposites, the water has no power over you. The fire is absolute master, subject to nothing. You will not be surprised, then, at my insistence through this book that you should strive to attain this freedom. Isn't it funny that a poor little nun of Saint Joseph's should attain mastery over the entire earth and all the elements? Do you wonder that the saints, with God's help, did whatever they wanted with these elements?. Fire and water obeyed Saint Martin, and even birds and fish were obedient to Saint Francis. Because they had worked so hard to despise the world and subjected themselves to the Lord of the world, they were masters over everything in the world. The water that springs from this earth has no power over this fire. Its flames rise high and its source is in nothing as base as the earth. There are other small fires of love for God which are quenched by little things. This fire, though, will certainly not be quenched. Even if an entire sea of temptations attacks it, they will not keep it from burning or prevent it from gaining mastery over them.

Water that comes down as rain from Heaven will not quench the flames either, for in this case water and fire have the same origin. Do not be afraid that one element may harm the other. Each helps the other, and they produce the same effect. The water of tears that comes from true prayer is a gift from the King of Heaven. It fans the flames and keeps them lighted while the fire helps to cool the water. What a beautiful and wonderful thing it is that fire should cool water. It even freezes all worldly affections when it is combined with the living water that comes from Heaven, the source of our tears. These tears are given to us; we do not acquire them through our diligence. Nothing worldly has enough warmth in it to urge us to cling to it unless it is something that increases this fire. This fire's nature is not easily satisfied; if possible, it engulfs the entire world.

The second property of water is that it cleanses unclean things. What would become of the world if there were no water for washing? Do you know what cleansing properties there are in this living water, this heavenly water, this clear water, when it is unclouded, free from mud, and comes down from Heaven? Once the soul has drunk of this water, it purifies and cleanses it of all its sins. God does not allow us to drink of this water of pure contemplation whenever we like. We do not have the choice. The Divine union is quite supernatural, given that it will purify and cleanse the soul from the mud and misery into which its sins have plunged it. Other comforts, however excellent, come through the understanding and are like water running all over the ground. Such water cannot be drunk directly from the source. Its course is never free from clogging impurities, and it is neither as clean nor as pure as the water from Heaven. This kind of prayer, which comes from reasoning with the intellect, is not living water. In spite of our efforts, the influence of our body and the baseness of our nature clings to our soul, even though we would prefer that it did not.

I will try to explain more. Sometimes when we are meditating on the transitory nature of the world so that we may learn to despise worldly things, we find ourselves reflecting, almost without noticing it, on the things in the world that we love. We try to dismiss these thoughts, but we cannot help thinking of things that have happened, or will happen, or of things we have done or are going to do. We then start thinking about how to get rid of such thoughts, but that sometimes immerses us again into the same danger. It is not necessary to omit such meditations,

but we need to maintain our misgivings about them
and not grow careless. When we contemplate, the
Lord Himself takes this care away from us, for He
will not trust us to look after ourselves. He loves our
souls so dearly that He prevents them from rushing
into things that may harm them just when He is
eager to help them. He calls these souls to His side
at once and reveals to them in a single moment more
truths and clearer insight into the nature of all things
than the souls could ever gain. For our sight is poor
and the dust on the road blinds us. In contemplation
the Lord brings us to the end of the day's journey
without our understanding how.

The third property of water is that it satisfies and
quenches thirst. Thirst means the desire for something so necessary that if we do not have it we will
die. It is strange that if we have no water we die and
that we can also lose our lives by having too much
water, as happens when people drown. My Lord, if
only one could plunge so deeply into this living
water that one's life would end. Can that be? Yes,
for this love and desire for God can increase so dra-
matically that human nature cannot bear it. I knew
one person who had such an abundance of this living water that she would almost have died in her
raptures if God had not helped her. She had such a
thirst, and her desire grew so greatly, that she realized
that she might possibly die of thirst, if something
were not done for her. In such a state the soul is tran-
quil and calm. Such a soul finds the world so intoler-

able that her soul is overwhelmed only to come to
life again in God.

Everything in our supreme Good is perfect.
Everything He gives us is for our welfare. No matter
how abundant this water is, He alone gives us the
water we need. If His gift is abundant, He also gives
to the soul an abundant drinking capacity. He is like
a glassmaker who molds his vessels so that there is
room for whatever he wishes to pour into them.
Since our desires for this water come from ourselves,
they are never free from fault. Any good there may
be in them comes from the help of the Lord. But,
since the pain is sweet and pleasant, we think we can
never allow ourselves to have too much of it. We
have an immeasurable longing for it and, as much as
it is possible on this earth, we stimulate this longing.
Sometimes this goes so far as to cause death. How
happy is such a death! Yet, by living one might have
helped others to die of the desire for it. I believe the
devil has something to do with this. Knowing how
much harm we can do him by living, he tempts us to
be indiscreet in our penances and thus ruin our
health.

I advise anyone who has an experience of this
fierce thirst to watch herself carefully, for she will
have to contend with such temptation. She may not
die of her thirst, but her health will be ruined. She
will involuntarily express her feelings outwardly,
something that should be avoided at all costs.
Sometimes, though, our diligence fails and we are

unable to hide our emotions as much as we would like. Whenever these strong impulses assault us, we should not succumb to them ourselves but arrest them by thinking of something else. Our own nature may have as great a part as love does in producing these feelings. There are some people like this who have keen desires for all kinds of things, even bad things. But, I do not think such people can have achieved great sacrifice, for sacrifice is always profitable. It seems foolish to halt this desire, but it is not. One may be able to arrest this desire by stimulating some other desire that is equally worthy of praise.

I will give you an illustration so you may understand me better. Like Saint Paul, a person possesses great desire to be with God and to be freed from this prison. This causes her pain that is in itself a great joy. She will need a great deal of sacrifice in order to arrest the desire, even though she will not always be able to do it. When she is so oppressed by this, she almost loses her reason. I saw this happen to someone once. She had an impetuous nature, but she was so accustomed to curbing her will that I thought she had completely destroyed her will. Yet when I saw her momentarily the great stress caused by her efforts to hide her feelings all but destroyed her reason. In such a case, I think, even if the Spirit of God was the source of the desire, it would be true humility to be afraid. We must not imagine that we have sufficient understanding to induce such a state of oppression.

I do not think it is wrong, then, for us to change our desire by reflecting that we have a better chance of serving God if we live. We might serve God by giving light to some soul that otherwise would be lost. If we serve Him more, we will deserve to enjoy him more and grieve that we have served Him so little. These are consolations suitable to such great trials. They will alleviate our pain and we will gain a great deal from them if, in order to serve the Lord, we are willing to spend a long time here below and to live with our grief. It is like a person's suffering a great trial or affliction and we console her by telling her to have patience and leave herself in God's hands so that His will might be fulfilled in her. It is always best to leave ourselves in God's hands.

What if the devil were responsible for these strong desires? This might be possible. Remember Cassian's story of the hermit. Though he led an austere life, the devil persuaded him to throw himself down a well so that he might see God sooner. I do not think this hermit could have served God humbly or efficiently, for the Lord is faithful and would never allow a servant of His to be blinded in a matter in which the truth was so clear. Of course, if this desire had come from God, it would have not harmed the hermit. Such desires bring illumination, moderation, and discretion with them. But our enemy seeks to harm us whenever he can. Since he always watches for an opportunity to harm us, we must always be careful to watch out for his wiles.

This is an important matter in many respects. For example, we must cut short our time of prayer, no matter how much joy it brings us, if we feel our bodily strength waning or that our head aches. Discretion is necessary in everything we do.

Why do you suppose that I have tried to describe the end of the battle and to point to its reward by telling you about the blessing that comes from drinking of the heavenly source of this living water? I have done this so the trials and annoyances of the road may not discourage you. I want you to walk this road with courage and not grow weary. It may be that, when you reach the end of the road and only have to stoop and drink from the spring, you may fail to do so and lose this blessing simply because you think you do not have the strength to do so.

Remember, the Lord invites us all. Since He is Truth Itself, we cannot doubt Him. If His invitation weren't general, He wouldn't have said, "If anyone thirsts, let him come to me and drink." He might have said: "Come, all of you, for after all you will lose nothing by coming, and I will give drink to those whom I think are fit to drink." However, since He said we were all to come, I feel sure that nobody will fail to receive this living water unless she cannot keep to the path. May the Lord give us grace to seek this path as it must be sought.

CHAPTER

20

With these remarks, I seem to be contradicting what I have already said. When I was trying to comfort those who had not reached the contemplative state, I told them that just as God has many mansions so there are many roads by which they can reach Him. God, understanding our weakness, has provided for us. But He did not say: "Some must come by this way and others by that way." His mercy is so great that He does not prohibit anyone from striving to come and drink of this fountain of life. Blessed be He forever, for He had good reasons for prohibiting me to complete this journey.

However, since He did not order me to stop drinking when I had begun to do so, but plunged me into deep water, surely He will not stop anyone from coming to drink. Indeed, He calls us publicly in a loud voice to do so. Yet, He is so good that He does not force us to drink. He enables those who want to follow Him to drink in many ways so that they will not lack comfort or die of thirst. Many streams flow from this rich spring. Some are large, some are small.

There are also little pools for children in the faith, for a great deal of water would frighten them. Do not be afraid of dying of thirst on this road. You will never lack so much of the water of comfort that your thirst will be intolerable. Take my advice and do not dawdle along the way. Strive like strong people until you die in the attempt, for you are here for no other reason than to strive. If you always pursue this determination to die rather than fail to reach this water, the Lord may bring you through this life with a certain degree of thirst. In the life which never ends, though, He will give you great abundance to drink and you will have no fear of its failing you. May the Lord grant that we never fail Him.

Let us consider how we should begin the first stage of our journey so that we will not go astray at the start. Every part of the journey is important to the whole. I don't mean that one who lacks a strong will and resolve should not set out on the journey, for the Lord will gradually bring her nearer to perfection. If she took no more than one step, the road alone has such virtue that she should not be afraid of losing the road or of failing to be rewarded. We might compare this person to someone who has a rosary with one bead larger than the rest that carries special indulgences for the souls in purgatory. One prayer in itself will bring her something, and the more she uses the bead, the more she will gain. But, if she left it in a box and never took it out, she would be better off not having it. Although she may never go any farther along the same road, the short distance she has progressed will give her light and thus help her to go along other roads. The farther she goes, the more light she will gain. She has not harmed herself by having started on the road, even if she leaves it, for good never leads to evil. Whenever you meet people who are well-disposed and attracted to the life of prayer, try to convince them not to be afraid of beginning a journey that will bring them such great blessings. For the love of God, I beg you always to see that your conversation benefits those with whom you speak. Your prayers must be for the profit of their souls. Since you must always pray for them, you would not be working for their good if you did not strive to benefit them in every possible way.

If you want to be a good relative, this is true friendship. If you want to be a good friend, you may be sure that this is the only possible way. If you practice meditation, you will have truth in your hearts, and you will see clearly the love we are bound to have for our neighbors. You must not use the phrases "If you love me," or "Don't you love me?" with either relatives or friends unless you have some noble end in view or hope to bring gain to the person to whom you're speaking. Sometimes you might need to use such phrases in order to get a relative to listen to the truth and accept it or to prepare him for it by using such phrases and showing him signs of love. He may possibly be more affected by one kind word than by a great deal you might say about God. There will be plenty of opportunities later to talk to your relative about God. I do not prohibit such phrases, then, as long as you use them to bring gain to someone. These phrases are good for no other reason, and they may even be harmful without your being aware of it. Everybody knows you are nuns whose business is prayer. Do not say to yourselves: "I have no wish to be considered good," for what people see in you will bring them either gain or harm. Let anyone who wants to talk to you learn your language. If they will not do so, then be careful never to learn theirs, for it might lead you to hell.

It doesn't matter if you are considered ill bred or if you are taken for hypocrites. You will gain by this because only those who understand your language will come to see you. Worldly people will not tire you nor harm you. You would be harmed by having to begin learning and talking a new language; you would spend all your time learning it. I have discovered through experience how bad this is for the soul. No sooner does one learn one thing than it has to forget another, and the soul never rests. On the road we are about to walk, peace and quiet are of great importance.

If those who come to see you want to learn your language, it is not your place to teach it to them. You can tell them what wealth they will gain by learning your language. Perform this task lovingly, piously, and prayerfully with a view toward helping them.

They will then realize what a great gain it brings, and they will go and seek a master to teach them. Our Lord would be doing you no light favor if He were to arouse some soul to obtain this blessing through your agency. When one begins to describe this road, what a large number of things can be said about it, even by those like me who have walked it so unsuccessfully. I only wish I could write with both hands, so as not to forget one thing while I am saying another. I hope it pleases the Lord, sisters, to be able to speak of it better than I have done.

CHAPTER

21

Don't be discouraged at the many things you must consider before setting out on this Divine journey, which is the royal road to Heaven. By taking this road we gain such precious treasures that it is no wonder that the cost is so high. Eventually we will realize that everything we have paid has been like nothing at all in comparison with the prize's greatness.

Let me talk some more about those who wish to travel on this road and will not stop until they have reached the place where they can drink of this water of life. They should begin well by determining not to stop until they reach this goal, no matter what happens to them, no matter how hard they have to work, and whether or not they have the devotion to endure the trials they meet. Yet, people will say over and over to us: "It is dangerous"; "So-and-so was lost through doing this"; "Someone else got into wrong ways"; "Some other person, who was always praying, fell just the same"; "It is bad for virtue"; "It is not meant for women; it may lead them into delusions"; "It is quite enough for them to say their Paternoster and Ave Maria."

I quite agree with this last remark. Of course it is enough. It is always a great thing to base your prayer on prayers that the Lord spoke with his own lips. People are quite right to say this. If our own devotion weren't so weak, we would not need any other systems of prayer or books. I am speaking to those who are unable to recollect themselves by meditating on the mysteries and who think they need special methods of prayer. Some people have such an ingenious mind that nothing is good enough for them. So, I will start to lay down some rules for each part of our prayer—beginning, middle, and end—though I will not spend much time on the higher stages.

I have always been fond of the words of the Gospels and have found more recollection in them than in the most carefully planned books. If I keep close to this Master of wisdom, perhaps He will give me some thoughts that will help you. I don't presume to explain these Divine prayers, for there are already a great many explanations of them. Even if there were none, it would be ridiculous for me to attempt such explanations. I will write down, though, a few thoughts on the words of the Paternoster. Sometimes when we are most anxious to nurture our devotion, consulting many books will kill it. When a teacher is giving a lesson, she treats her student kindly, hoping the student likes learning and doing everything she can to help her student learn. The heavenly Teacher treats us in just this way.

Don't pay attention to those who try to frighten you by portraying the dangers of the way. What a strange idea that one could expect to travel on a thief-infested road, with the purpose of gaining a great treasure, without encountering dangers. Worldly people like to take life peaceably. However, these people will rob themselves of sleep to make money, and such riches give you neither peace of body nor peace of soul. Even if some people try to frighten you while you are on the safe road walked by our King, His elect, and His saints, how much greater are the dangers encountered by those who think they will be able to gain this treasure and yet are not on this royal road?

How much greater are the risks that these worldly people run. They are not even aware of these risks until they fall recklessly into some real danger. Since they may have no one to help them, they lose this water altogether and never drink from it. How can they get along without even a drop of this water and still travel along a road on which they encounter so many enemies? Sooner or later they will die of thirst. We must all journey to this fountain, whether we want to or not, though we may not make the journey in the same way. Take my advice, then, and do not let anybody mislead you by showing you any other road other than the road of prayer.

I am not now discussing whether or not everyone must practice mental or vocal prayer. You need both. Prayer is the duty of the religious. If anyone tells you prayer is dangerous, you must see that person as your main danger and run from his company. Do not forget this, for it is advice that you might need. If you do not possess humility and the other virtues, you will be in danger. God forbid, though, that the way of prayer be a way of danger. Such a fear seems to have been invented by the devil, who has very cleverly brought about the fall of some who practice prayer.

The world is very blind, for it does not consider the thousands who have fallen into heresies and other great evils by yielding to distractions and not practicing prayer. Out of these multitudes there are a few who did practice prayer and whom the devil has been successful enough to seduce. By doing this he has also made some people afraid of virtuous practices. Let those who use this excuse to absolve themselves from such practices be careful, for in order to save themselves they are fleeing from good. I have never heard of such a wicked invention. It must indeed come from the devil. Oh, my Lord, defend Yourself. Look at the way Your words are being misunderstood. Permit no such weakness in Your servants.

There is one great blessing: You will always find a few people ready to help you. The true servant of God, to whom the Lord has given light to follow the true path, only grows more determined to reach her goal when she is confronted with these fears. She sees clearly from which side the devil's blows are coming, but she evades each blow and breaks her adversary's head. The anger this arouses in the devil is greater than all the satisfaction he receives from all the pleasures others give him. When the devil seems to be leading people anywhere he wants to and deceiving them into believing that they are zealous for the right, God raises up someone to open their eyes and see the fog with which the devil has shrouded their path. How great God is! To think that one or two people can do more by telling the truth than can a great many people together. They gradually begin to see the path again and God gives them courage. If people say there is a danger in prayer, this servant of God, by her deeds if not by her words, tries to make them realize what a good thing prayer is. If they say that frequent communion is inadvisable, she only practices it more. Thus, because just one or two are following the better path, the Lord gradually regains what He had lost.

Stop worrying about these fears, then, and never pay attention to such matters of popular opinion. This is no time for believing everyone. Believe only those who model their lives on Christ's life. Strive always to have a good conscience. Practice humility. Despise all worldly things. Believe firmly in the teaching of our Holy Mother Church. You may then be quite sure you are on a very good road. Stop being afraid of things of which there is no fear. If anyone tries to frighten you, point out the truth in all humility. Tell him that you have a Rule that commands you to pray without ceasing and that you must keep that rule. If they tell you that you should practice only vocal prayer, ask whether your mind and heart should not be in what you say. If they answer "Yes," they are admitting that you are bound to practice mental prayer and even contemplation, if God should grant it to you.

CHAPTER

22

You must know that whether or not you are practicing mental prayer has nothing to do with keeping your lips closed. If, while I am speaking with God, I am fully conscious of doing so, and if this is more real to me than the words I am uttering, then I am combining mental and vocal prayer. I am amazed when people tell that you are speaking with God by reciting the Paternoster even while you are thinking of worldly things. When you speak with a Lord so great, you should think of Who it is you are addressing and what you yourself are, if only that you may speak to Him with proper respect. How can you address a king with the reverence he deserves unless you are clearly conscious of his position and of yours?

How is it, My Lord, that You can tolerate this, Prince of all Creation? For You, my God, are a King without end, and Yours is no borrowed Kingdom, but Your own, and it will never pass away. When the Creed says, "Whose Kingdom shall have no end" the phrase nearly always makes me feel particularly happy. I praise You, Lord, and bless You, for Your

Kingdom will endure forever. Never allow those who praise You with their lips alone, Lord, to think that this is right. What do you mean, Christians, when you say that mental prayer is unnecessary? Do you understand what you are saying? I really don't think you can. So, you want us all to go wrong. You cannot know what mental prayer is, or how vocal prayers should be said, or what contemplation means. If you knew this, you would not condemn on the one hand what you praise on the other.

Whenever I remember to do so, I will always speak of mental and vocal prayer together so that you will not be alarmed. I know where such fears lead, for I have suffered a certain number of trials in this respect. I would be sorry if anyone unsettled you, for it very bad for you to have misgivings while you are walking on this path. It is important for you to realize you are making progress. If someone tells a traveler that she has taken the wrong road and lost her way, she begins to wander aimlessly. The constant search for the right road tires her, wastes her time, and delays her arrival. Who can say it is wrong if, before we begin reciting the Hours of the Rosary, we think Whom we are addressing and who we are in addressing Him, so we may do so in the way we should? If you consider deeply these two points before beginning your vocal prayers you will be engaging in mental prayer for a very long time. For we cannot approach a prince and address him in the same way we talk to a peasant.

The reason we sometimes do so can be explained by this King's humility. Even though I am unskilled in speaking with Him, He does not refuse to hear me or forbid me to approach Him or command His guards to throw me out. The angels in His presence know well that their King prefers the unskilled language of a humble peasant to the speech of the wisest and most learned people, no matter how elegant their arguments, if this speech is not humble. But, we must not be rude because He is good. If only to show our gratitude to Him for allowing someone like me to come near him, we should try to realize His purity and His nature.

O You, our Emperor! Supreme Power, Supreme Goodness, Wisdom Itself, without beginning, without end and without measure in Your works: These are infinite and incomprehensible, a fathomless ocean of wonders, O Beauty containing within Yourself all beauties. O Very Strength! O God, help me! I wish I could command all the eloquence of mortals and all wisdom to understand that to know nothing is everything and thus to describe some of the many things on which we may meditate in order to learn something of our Lord's nature.

When you approach God, try to realize Whom you are about to address and continue to do so while you are addressing Him. If you had a thousand lives, you would never fully understand why this Lord deserves our behavior toward Him, before Whom even the angels tremble. He orders all things

and He can do all things; with Him to will is to perform. We should rejoice in these wondrous qualities
of our Spouse and to know Whom we have wedded
and what our lives should be. When a woman in this
world is about to marry, she knows beforehand
whom she is to marry, what kind of person he is,
and what property he possesses. Shouldn't we, then,
who are already engaged, think about our Spouse
before we marry Him and He takes us home to be
with Him? If such thoughts are not forbidden in the
world, how can we be forbidden to discover Who
this Man is, Who is His Father, what is the country
to which He will take us, what are the riches with
which He promises to endow me, what is His rank,
how I can best make Him happy, what I can do that
will give Him pleasure.

Shall people pay less respect to You, my Spouse,
than to men? If they think it is unfitting to honor
You, let them at least leave You Your brides, who
are to spend their lives with You. A woman is indeed
fortunate in her life if her husband is so jealous that
he will not allow her to speak with anyone but him.
It would be a pretty pass if she could not decide to
give him this pleasure, for it is reasonable enough
that she should submit to this and not wish to talk
to anyone else, since in him she has all she can desire.
To understand these truths is to understand mental
prayer. If you wish to understand them and, at the
same time, to practice vocal prayer, well and good.
But do not address God while you are thinking of

other things, for to do so is not to understand the nature of mental prayer. I think I have made this clear. May the Lord help us to learn how to put it into practice.

There are so many reasons we should be determined from the start that if I were to list them all I would have to write many books. I will tell you just two or three of these reasons. One is that when we decide to give anything to Him Who has given us so much, and Who is continually giving, it would be wrong for us not to be dedicated entirely to Him and to act like someone who lends something and expects to get it back. I do not call this "giving." Anyone who has been lent something feels displeased when the lender wants it back, especially if she is using it herself and thinks of it as her own. If the two are friends and the lender is indebted to the recipient for many things she has given her freely, the recipient will think it is mean and a lack of good will if the lender will not leave her even the smallest thing, even as a sign of love.

What wife will not give her husband, who has given her many valuable jewels, a ring as a sign of love and a token that she will be his until she dies? Does the Lord deserve so much less than this that we should mock Him by taking away the worthless gift we have given Him? Since we have made up our minds to devote this brief period of time to Him—only a small part of which we spend upon ourselves and upon people who are not especially grateful to us for it—let us give it to Him freely with our minds unoccupied by other things. We should make up our minds not to take back the time we have committed to Him, no matter what kinds of trials or annoyances we suffer. Let me realize that this time is being lent to me and it is not my own. I can rightly be called to account for this time if I am not prepared to devote it entirely to God.

However, if we fail to give Him this time for a day or two because of a legitimate occupation or an illness, we cannot be thought to be taking back this time. My God is not the least meticulous about such matters, as long as the intention remains firm. He does not look at trivial details. If you are trying to please Him in any way, He will certainly accept that as your gift. The other way is suitable for ungenerous souls, so mean that they are not capable of giving but lending only. Let these souls make some effort, though, for our Lord will judge everything we do to our credit and accept everything we want to give Him. As He judges us, He is not exacting, but generous. No matter how large the amount we owe Him, it is a small thing for Him to forgive us. As to our payment, He is so careful that you need have no fear He will leave us without our reward if only we raise our eyes to Heaven and remember Him.

The second reason we should have strong resolve is that such determination will give the devil less opportunity to tempt us. He is very afraid of determined souls, knowing from experience that they injure him greatly. When he plans to harm them, he only benefits them and others and is himself the loser. We must be careful. We have to deal with dangerous and deceptive people who are cowardly and do not attack the watchful. If they see we are careless, though, they will try to do us great harm. If they know anyone is wavering in her determination, they will bother her continually and suggest to her endless doubts and misgivings. I know these things very well from my own experience.

Another reason is that a determined person fights more courageously. She knows that whatever comes her way she must not retreat. She is like a soldier in battle who is aware that if he is conquered his life will not be spared and that if he escapes death in battle he must die afterwards. Such a soldier will fight much more courageously and will fear the enemy's blows the less because he understands the importance of victory. We must be firmly convinced that if we fight courageously and do not allow ourselves to be beaten, we will get what we want. No matter how small our gains, they will make us very rich. Do not be afraid that the Lord Who has called us to drink of this spring will allow us to die of thirst. I have already said this, but I must repeat it. People are often timid when they have not directly experienced the Lord's goodness, even though they know it by faith. It is wonderful to have experienced the friendship and joy He gives to those who walk on this road and how He takes almost the entire cost of it upon Himself.

It is not surprising that those who have not been tested in such a way should want to be sure that they will receive some gain for their effort. You already know, though, that even in this life we will receive a great profit and that the Lord says, "Ask and it will be given to you." If you do not believe the Lord in those passages of His Gospel where He gives us this assurance, it won't do you much good for me to keep telling you about it. Still, anyone who is in doubt will not lose anything by putting the matter to the test. This journey has the advantage of giving us much more than we ask for or will ever get. This is a truth that never fails. I can call as witnesses those of you who, by God's goodness, know it from experience.

L et me speak some more about those souls who
cannot practice recollection or mental prayer
or meditation. We must not say anything to
them about either of these two latter things, for they
will not listen. Indeed, a great many people seem ter-
rified at the very mention of contemplation or mental prayer.

I want to teach you how to practice vocal prayer
in case you meet someone like this, for you need to
understand what kinds of things you are saying.
Anyone who is not able to keep her mind on God
will find herself exhausted by long prayers. Thus, I
will not discuss such prayers. Instead, I will speak
simply about prayers that as Christians we recite as
a matter of course, specifically, the Paternoster and
the Ave Maria. Then no one will be able to accuse us
of repeating words without understanding what we
are saying. Of course, we may think it is a sufficient
habit to repeat the words of our prayers. However, I
would like for us not to be satisfied with this alone.
When I say the Creed, it seems right to me that I
should understand and know what it is I believe.

When I repeat the "Our Father," I think it should be a matter of love for me to understand Who this Father is. It will be well, too, for us to see Who the Master is who teaches us this prayer.

If we assert that it is sufficient to know once and for all Who the Master is, without thinking of Him again, you might equally say that it is sufficient to recite the prayer once in a lifetime. But there is a great deal of difference between one master and another. It would be wrong for us not to think about those who teach us, even on earth. If they are holy men and spiritual masters, and we are good pupils, it is impossible for us not to love them greatly, honor them deeply, and talk about them often. When it comes to the Master Who taught us this prayer, and Who loves us so much that He hopes we gain from His love, may God forbid that we fail to think of Him when we repeat the prayer.

In the first place, you know that Our Lord teaches that we should pray this prayer when we are alone, just as He was often alone when He prayed. It is impossible to speak to God and to the world at the same time. Yet, this is just what we are trying to do when we are saying our prayers and listening to others' conversations or letting our thoughts wander, without trying to control them. There are times when one cannot help this: times of sickness, times when our heads are tired and, no matter how hard we try, we cannot concentrate, or times when, for their own good, God allows His servants to suffer for days on end. Although they are distressed, they are not able to pay attention to what they are saying, no matter how hard they try.

Anyone who is suffering in this manner should not worry, for she is not to blame. She should pray as best she can. Indeed, she does not need to pray at all, but she should try to rest her spirit and make herself busy with some virtuous action. These instructions are directed to people who know that they cannot speak to God and the world at the same time. What we can do is try to be alone. May God grant that this is sufficient to make us realize Whose presence we are in and how the Lord answers our prayers. Do you think that because we cannot hear Him, He is silent? He speaks clearly to the heart when we beg Him from our hearts to do so. It would be a good idea for us to imagine that He has taught this prayer to each one of us individually and that He is continually teaching it to us. The Master is never so far away that the disciple needs to shout to be heard. He is always right at our side. If you want to recite the Paternoster well, you must not leave the side of the Master Who taught it to you.

You will complain that this is meditation, you are incapable of it, and that you are content with vocal prayer. There are impatient people who do not like to trouble themselves, and it is troublesome to practice meditation when one has not made it a habit. In order not to tire themselves, they say they are incapable of anything but vocal prayer and do not know how to do anything more. You are right that I have described mental prayer, but I cannot distinguish it from vocal prayer faithfully recited with a realization of Who it is we are addressing. We should try to pray attentively. May God grant that, by using these means, we may learn to say the Paternoster well and not find ourselves thinking of irrelevant thoughts while we are reciting it. When this happens to me, I have found that the best remedy is to fix my mind on the Person Who first spoke the words. Have patience and try to make this necessary practice into a habit.

CHAPTER
25

In case you think there isn't much to gain by practicing vocal prayer perfectly, I must tell you that while you are repeating the Paternoster or some other vocal prayer, the Lord might quite possibly grant you perfect contemplation. In this way our Lord shows He is listening to the person speaking to Him. In His greatness He is speaking to her, suspending her understanding, and taking the words out of her mouth so she cannot speak even if she wants to.

This person understands through such silence that the Divine Master is teaching her by suspending her faculties. If her mind's faculties were to work, they would be causing her more harm than help. The understanding rejoices without knowing how it rejoices. The soul is enflamed with love without understanding how it loves. It knows that it is rejoicing in the object of its love, yet it does not know how it is rejoicing in it. The soul is well aware that this is a joy that cannot be reached by the understanding. The will embraces this joy, without understanding how. However, the soul does understand that this joy is a blessing that could not be gained by all the merits of all the trials suffered on earth. It is a gift from the Lord of Heaven and earth, Who freely gives it like the God He is. This is perfect contemplation.

You see now how different this contemplation is from mental prayer. Such prayer involves thinking about what we are saying, understanding it, realizing to Whom we are speaking, and asking ourselves how we dare to speak to so great a Lord. To think about these kinds of things and others, like how little we have served Him and how great an obligation we have to serve Him, is mental prayer. Don't let the name frighten you. Vocal prayer involves reciting the Paternoster and the Ave Maria or any other petition you like. Think, though, of how harsh your music will sound if it lacks what must come first. Sometimes you will even get the words in the wrong order. With God's help, we may accomplish something ourselves in these two kinds of prayer. In contemplation we can do nothing ourselves. Our Lord does everything. The work is His alone and far transcends human nature.

Since I have already written a great deal about contemplation, I will not repeat myself here. I am ashamed to tell you that people make much use of anything of mine, and the Lord knows with what confusion I write a great deal of what I do write. Blessed be He for bearing with me. Let those who have not experienced supernatural prayer leave everything to the Lord, to Whom it belongs to grant this gift. He will not deny it to those who are striving with all their might to reach the end of their journey.

CHAPTER 26

Let us discuss vocal prayer some more so that we may learn to pray in such a way that, without our understanding how, God may give us everything at once. If we do this, we will be praying as we ought to be praying. As you know, the first things you do must be to examine your conscience, confess your sins, and sign yourselves with the Cross. Then you must look for a companion. Who could be a better Companion than the Master Who taught you the prayer you are about to say? Imagine that this Lord Himself is at your side and look at how lovingly and humbly He teaches you. You should stay with such a good Friend for as long as you can before you leave Him. If you get used to having Him at your side, and if He sees that you love Him to be there and are always trying to please Him, you will never be able to send Him away and He will never fail you. He will help you in all your trials and you will have Him everywhere. It is a great thing to have such a Friend beside you.

Those of you who cannot focus your constantly wandering thoughts on God must at all costs form this habit. I know you are capable of it. I also know that the Lord will help you if you approach Him humbly and ask Him to be with you. If an entire year passes without your obtaining what you ask for, you should be prepared to continue asking. You should never complain about time so well spent. It is possible to form the habit of walking at this true Master's side.

I am not asking you to become involved in long and subtle meditations with your understanding and reason. I am only asking you to look at Him. Who can prevent you from turning the eyes of your soul upon this Lord? You can look at very ugly things; can't you, then, look at the most beautiful thing imaginable? Your Spouse never takes his eyes off you. He has endured patiently thousands of foul and abominable sins you have committed against Him, yet even your sins have not been enough to make Him turn His eyes away from you. Is it so hard for you to look away from outward things sometimes and to look at Him? He is only waiting for us to look at Him. If you want Him, you will find Him. He yearns so much for us to look at Him that it will not be a lack of effort on His part if we fail to do so.

They say that a wife must be like this if she is to have a happy married life with her husband. If he is sad, she must show signs of sadness. If he is joyous, then she must appear to be joyous, even if she is herself not joyous. This is how we are treated by the Lord. He becomes subject to us and is pleased to let you be His mistress and to conform to your will. If you are happy, look upon your risen Lord, and the very thought of how He rose from the grave will gladden you. How bright and beautiful He was then. How majestic. How victorious. How joyful. He was like someone emerging from a battle in which He had gained a great kingdom, all of which He desires you to possess. Is it really so hard to turn your eyes just once and look upon Him Who has given you such gifts?

If you are suffering trials, or are sad, look upon Him on His way to the Garden. What terrible distress He must have carried in His soul, to describe His own suffering as He did and not to complain about it. Or look upon Him on the Cross, full of pain, His flesh torn to pieces by His great love for you. How much He suffered: persecuted by some, spit upon by others, denied by His friends with no one to defend Him, frozen with the cold, left completely alone. Look upon Him bending under the weight of the Cross and not even allowed to breathe. He looks upon you with His lovely and compassionate eyes, full of tears. In comforting your grief He will forget His own because you are bearing Him company in order to comfort Him and turning your head to look upon Him.

"O Lord of the world, my true Spouse," you may say to Him. Seeing Him in such a condition has filled your heart with such tenderness that you not only desire to look upon Him but love to speak to

Him. You do not use the forms of prayer, but use words that come from the compassion of your heart, which means so much to Him: "Are You so needy, my Lord and my Good, that You will accept poor companionship like mine? Do I read in Your face that You have found comfort, even in me? How can it be possible, Lord, that the angels are leaving You alone and that Your Father is not comforting You?"

"Lord, if You are willing to suffer all this for me, what am I suffering for You? What do I have to complain about? I am ashamed, Lord, when I see You in such a situation. If there is any way I can imitate You I will suffer all trials that come to my way and count them as a great blessing. Lord, let us go together; wherever You go, I must go, and I must pass through whatever You pass." Take up this cross. Don't pay any attention if people mock you if you can only save Him from some of His trials. Stumble and fall with your Spouse but do not give up your cross. Think often about how tired He was on His journey and how much harder His trials were than the ones you have to suffer. No matter how hard you think your trials are or how much affliction you think they cause you, they will be a source of comfort to you. For you will disdain your trials when you compare them with His trials.

You will ask me how you can possibly do all these things. You will also say that if you had seen our Lord with your bodily eyes when He was living in the world, you would have gazed at Him forever.

Do not believe it. Anyone who will not make the effort to gaze upon this Lord present within her, which she can do with little trouble or danger, would not be likely to have stood at the foot of the Cross with the Magdalen, who looked death straight in the face. What the glorious Virgin and this blessed saint must have suffered. What threats, what malicious words, what shocks, what insults. The people they were dealing with were not exactly polite to them. No, theirs was the kind of courtesy you might meet in hell, for they were the devil's ministers. Yet, as terrible as the sufferings of these women must have been, they would not have noticed them even in the presence of much greater pain.

Don't suppose, then, that you would have been prepared to endure such great trials then, if you are not ready to endure such trifling ones now. If you practice enduring these trifling ones now, you may be given greater ones. You will find it very helpful if you can get a picture of this Lord to use regularly when you talk to Him. He will tell you what to say. If you don't have trouble talking to people on earth, why should you have trouble talking to God? Words will not fail you if you form the habit of talking. If you never talk to a person, she soon becomes a stranger and you forget how to talk to her. Before long, even if she is a relative, you will feel like you don't know her. Both family and friends lose their influence when you stop talking to them.

It might also help to have a good book, written in

simple language, to help you in your prayer habits. With such an aid you will learn your vocal prayers well, and little by little your soul will get used to this. Many years have passed since the soul fled from its Spouse, and it needs careful handling before it will return home. We sinners are like that. Our souls and minds are so accustomed to seek their own pleasures until the unfortunate soul no longer knows what it is doing. When that has happened, a good deal of skill is necessary before it can be inspired with enough love to make it stay home. Unless we gradually do this, though, we will not accomplish anything. If you carefully form the kinds of habits I have been writing about, you will gain so much profit from them that I could not describe it even if I wanted to. Stay at this good Master's side, and be determined to learn what He teaches you. The Lord will be sure that you do not fail to be good disciples, and He will never leave you unless you leave Him. Think about those words spoken by the Divine lips: The very first of them will show you at once how much love He has for you. It is a great blessing and joy for the student to see how much her Master loves her.

CHAPTER
27

"Our Father, which art in the Heavens." My Lord, how fittingly You reveal Yourself as the father of such a Son. How fittingly Your Son reveals Himself as the Son of such a Father. May You be blessed forever and ever. Shouldn't a favor as great as this one come at the end of the prayer? Here at the beginning You fill our hands and grant us so great a favor that it would be a great blessing if our understanding could be filled and our will occupied. We would thus be unable to say another word. How appropriate perfect contemplation would be here. How right the soul would be to enter into itself, so it could rise above itself and so that this holy Son might show it the nature of the place where He says His Father dwells—in the Heavens. Let us leave earth, for it is not right that such a favor should be valued so little.

How can You give us so much with Your first word, O Son of God and my Lord? It is wonderful that You should descend to such a degree of humility to join with us when we pray and to become the Brother of such lowly and miserable creatures. How can You give us, in the name of Your Father, all that there is to be given by willing Him to have us as His children? You oblige Him to fulfill His word. This is no light task since, being our Father, He must bear with us no matter how great our sins are. If we return to Him, as did the prodigal son, He must pardon us. He must comfort us in our trials, and He must sustain us as such a Father is bound to do. For He is better than any earthly father, since everything has its perfection in Him. He must cherish us; He must sustain us; at the last He must make us participants and fellow-heirs with You.

My Lord, with the love You have for us and with Your humility, nothing can be an obstacle to You. You have lived on the earth and have clothed Yourself in our humanity. You thus have a reason to care about our good. But, as You have told us, Your Father is in Heaven, and You should consider His honor. Since You have offered Yourself to be dishonored by us, leave Your Father free. Do not ask Him to do so much for wicked people like me, who will be poor examples for Him.

You have shown clearly that You are One with Him and that Your will is His and His is Yours. What an open confession this is, my Lord. What is this love that You have for us? You deceived the devil by concealing from him Your identity as the Son of God. Your great desire for our welfare overcomes all obstacles to Your granting us this great favor. Who but You could do this, Lord? I can't understand how the devil failed to understand from Your word Who You were. I see clearly that You spoke both as a dearly beloved son on Your behalf and on our behalf. You have such power that what You say in Heaven will also be done on earth. Blessed be You forever, my Lord, Who love to give so much that no obstacles can prevent You from doing so.

Don't you think our Master is good, since He begins by granting us this great favor to make us love to learn what He has to teach us? Do you think it would be right for us to stop trying to think of what we are saying while we are repeating this prayer with our lips just because picturing such love would tear our hearts to pieces? Anyone who realized His greatness would not ask such a question. What son would not try to learn his father's identity if he had one as good as ours? If God were not all these things it would not surprise me if we did not want to be known as His children.

O College of Christ, in which the Lord was pleased that Saint Peter, a fisherman, had more authority than Saint Bartholomew, the son of a king. Our Lord knew what a fuss would be made about who was fashioned from the finer clay. Dear Lord, we make such trouble about these things. God deliver us from such arguments, even if they are carried on only in fun. I hope that our Lord will indeed deliver you. If any such strife happens among you, let the person concerned be afraid, for it is like having Judas among the

Apostles. Do what you can to get rid of such a bad companion. If you cannot get rid of her, give her penances heavier than anything else until she realizes that she has not deserved to be even the basest clay. The good Jesus gives you a good Father. Strive to lead such a life that you deserve to find comfort in Him and to throw yourselves into His arms. If you are good children, He will never send you away. Who would do anything they could rather than lose such a Father?

Thank God that there is great cause for comfort here. I will let you think about all these things. No matter how much Your thoughts may wander between such a Son and such a Father the Holy Spirit will come to you. May He enflame your will and bind You to Himself with fervent love.

CHAPTER 28

Reflect now upon what the Master says next in His prayer: "Who are in the Heavens." Do you think it really matters what Heaven is and where you must look for your most holy Father? For minds that wander it is of great importance not only to have a right belief but to try to learn it by experience, for this is one of the very best ways of concentrating your thoughts.

You know that God is everywhere. This is a great truth, for wherever God is, there is Heaven. You can believe that in any place where our Lord resides, there is fullness of glory. Recall that Saint Augustine tells us about his seeking God in many places and eventually finding Him within himself. A soul that is often distracted needs to understand this truth, for in order to speak to its Eternal Father and to take its delight in Him, it has no need to go to Heaven or to speak in a loud voice. No matter how quietly we speak, He is so near that He will hear us. We do not need wings to search for Him. We only need to find a place where we can be alone and look upon Him present within us. We don't need to feel strange in the presence of such a kind Guest. We must talk very humbly to Him, as we should to our father, ask Him for things as we should ask a father, tell Him our troubles, beg Him to correct them, and realize that we are not worthy to be called His children.

Do not confuse modesty with God as humility. You would not be humble if God were to do you a favor and you refused to accept it. You would be showing humility by accepting it, being pleased with it, yet realizing how far you are from deserving it. A fine humility it would be if I had the Emperor of Heaven and earth in my house, coming to it to do me a favor, and I were so humble that I would not answer His questions, sit with Him, or accept what He gave me, but left Him alone.

Rather than having that kind of humility, speak to Him as with a Father, a Brother, a Lord, and a Spouse. He will teach you what you need to do to please Him. Do not be foolish. Ask Him to let you speak to Him. Remember how important it is to understand that the Lord is within us and that we should be there with Him.

If you pray in this way, the prayer may be only vocal, but the mind will enter into the prayer much sooner. This is a prayer that brings a thousand blessings with it. It is called recollection because the soul collects all the faculties together and enters within itself to be with its God. Its Divine Master comes more speedily to teach it and to grant it the Prayer of Quiet. Hidden there within itself, it can think about the Passion and picture the Son without tiring the mind by going to seek Him on Calvary, or in the Garden, or on the Cross.

Those who are able to shut themselves up in this little Heaven of the soul, wherein the Maker of Heaven and earth dwells, and who have formed the habit of looking at nothing and staying in no place that distracts the senses, may be sure that they are walking on an excellent road. They will not fail to drink of the water of the fountain, for they will travel a long way in a short time. They are like travelers on a ship who, with a little good wind, reach the end of their voyage in a few days, while those who travel by land take much longer to arrive.

These souls have already put out to sea. Although they are not yet out of sight of land, they do what they can to get away from it, by recollecting their senses. If their recollection is genuine, it produces certain effects which I cannot explain, but which anyone will recognize from their experience of them. It is as if the soul were rising from play, for it sees that worldly things are nothing but toys. In time, then, the soul rises above them, like a person entering a castle, so that it has nothing more to fear from its enemies. It withdraws the senses from all outward things and rejects them so completely that its eyes close and it cannot see them. Thus, the soul's spiritual sight becomes clear. Those who walk along this path almost always close their eyes when they say their prayers. This is an admirable custom, since it means they are trying not to look at the things of the world. The soul seems to gather up its strength and to master itself at the body's expense, which it leaves weakened and alone. In this way, the soul becomes stronger for the fight against it.

This may not be evident at first, if the recollection is not very profound. At first it may cause a good deal of trouble, for the body insists on its rights. It doesn't understand that if it refuses to admit defeat it is cutting off its own head. If we cultivate the habit, make the necessary effort, and practice the exercises for several days, we will see the benefits. When we begin to pray we will realize that the bees are coming to the hive and entering it make honey, all without any effort of ours. It is the Lord's will that the soul and the will should be given power over the senses. They will only have to make a sign to show that they wish to enter into recollection and the senses will obey and allow themselves to be recollected. They may come out at some later time. However, it is a great thing for them to have surrendered, for if they come out as captives and slaves they will not do as much harm as they might have done before. When the will calls them, they respond more quickly. After they have entered the soul many times, the Lord is pleased that they should remain there in perfect contemplation.

Although all this seems obscure, anyone who wants to put it into practice can understand it. The sea voyage can be made. We should not travel too slowly. We need to consider the ways we can get accustomed to these good habits. Souls who do so are more protected from many occasions of sin, and the fire of Divine love is more readily ignited in them. They are so near the fire that, however little the understanding has fanned the flames, any small spark that flies out at them will cause them to burst into flame. When it is not hindered from the outside, the soul remains alone with its God and is thoroughly prepared to be ignited.

Let us imagine that we have within us a palace built of gold and precious stones fit for so great a Lord. Imagine that you are partially responsible for the beauty of the palace. There is no building so beautiful as a soul that is pure and full of virtues; the greater these virtues are, the more brilliantly the stones shine. Imagine that within the palace dwells this great King, Who has come down to be your Father, and Who sits upon a throne of supreme price—your heart.

This point may seem irrelevant, but it may eventually prove useful. We need all these things to help us realize that we actually have something within us that is incomparably more precious than anything we see outside. Don't think that the interior of the soul is empty. If we were careful always to remember what a Guest we have within us, I think it would be impossible for us to abandon ourselves to vanities and things of this world. We would see how worthless they are compared with those which we have inside us. When an animal seizes whatever attracts him when he sees it, isn't he merely satisfying his hunger? There should surely be a difference between the brute beasts and us, since we have such a Father. You will probably laugh at me and say how obvious such things are. But, until I closed my eyes to the vanities of this world, I did not see or understand Who lived within my soul or what my soul deserved. If I had understood then, as I now do, how this great King lives within this palace of my soul, I would not have left Him alone so much. I would have stayed with Him and not let His house get so dirty. It is wonderful that He Whose greatness could fill a thousand worlds should confine Himself to so small a space, just as He was pleased to inhabit His most holy Mother's womb. As our Lord, He has perfect freedom, and because He loves us, He fashions Himself to our measure.

When a soul sets out on this path, He does not reveal Himself to it. If the Lord did so, the soul might be daunted by seeing that its littleness can contain such greatness. Gradually He enlarges it to the extent needed for what He has to set within it. Thus, He has perfect freedom, for He has the power to make the entire palace great. We should be determined to give it to Him for His own and should empty it so that He may take out and put in whatever He likes. Our Lord is right in demanding this; let us not deny it to Him. He refuses to force our will. He takes what we give Him but does not give

Himself wholly until He sees that we are giving ourselves entirely to Him. He likes everything to be
done in order. If we fill the palace with vulgar people and all kinds of junk, how can the Lord and His
Court occupy it? When such a crowd fills the palace,
it would be a great thing if He were to remain even
for a short time.

Do you think He is alone when He comes to us?
Don't you know that His most holy Son says: "Who
are in the Heavens"? His attendants would not
abandon such a King. They stay with Him and pray
to Him on our behalf and for our welfare, for they
are full of charity. Heaven is not like this earth
where, if a king shows favors to anyone, people at
once become envious. Though the king has done
nothing to them, they treat him maliciously.

CHAPTER
29

For the love of God, daughters, avoid making such a big fuss about such favors. You should do your duty, and if this is not appreciated by your superior, you may be sure that the Lord will appreciate it and reward. We did not come here to seek rewards in this life, but only in the life to come. Let our thoughts be fixed on the things that endure and do not trouble yourselves with earthly things, which do not endure, even for a lifetime. Some other sister might be in the superior's good books, but tomorrow, if she sees you exhibiting some additional virtue, she may be better pleased with you. Do not allow such thoughts to develop; they will make you very uncomfortable. Put a stop to such thoughts by remembering that your kingdom is not of this world. Everything comes quickly to an end, and there is nothing in this life that goes on without changes.

Even this is not a completely perfect remedy. It is best that you should be humbled and out of favor. You should wish this to be so for the sake of the Lord Who lives within you. Turn your eyes upon

yourself and look at yourself inwardly. You will find
your Master, and He will not fail you. The less outward comfort you have, the greater joy He will give
you. He is full of compassion and never fails those
who are afflicted and out of favor if they trust in
Him alone. David tells us that he never saw the just
forsaken and that the Lord is with the afflicted.
Either you believe this or you do not: If you do, why
do you worry so much?

If we really knew you, Lord, we should not make
such a fuss about anything, because You give so
much to those who will give You their whole trust.
It is great to realize the truth of this so we may see
how deceptive earthly things and favors are when
they keep the soul from its course and keep it from
entering within itself. God help me! I owe You more
than anyone else but even I cannot grasp this as well
as I should be able to do.

I would like to be able to explain this holy companionship with our great Companion, the Holiest
of the holy, in which there is nothing to stop the soul
and her Spouse from remaining alone together.
There is nothing to stop her from shutting the door
behind her so as to keep out worldly things and to
live in Paradise with her God. There is nothing to
stop her from entering within herself when she so
desires. This is not a supernatural state, but it
depends upon our own will. By God's favor, we can
enter it of our own accord. We must understand this
condition if everything we say in this book can be

done. Without the will nothing can be accomplished and we do not have the power to think a single good thought. This is not a silence of the faculties; the soul encloses the faculties within itself.

There are many ways we can gradually acquire this habit. We must throw aside everything else in order to approach God inwardly. We must retire within ourselves, even during our ordinary occupations. It helps me to recall the companionship I have within my soul. We should know and abide with the Person with Whom we are speaking and not turn our backs on Him. We turn our backs on Him when we talk to God and think of all kinds of vain things. The whole problem comes from our not grasping the fact that He is near us and imagining Him so far away that we will have to go to Heaven to find Him. How is it, Lord, that we do not look at Your face when it is so near to us? We do not think people are listening to us when we are speaking to them unless we see them looking at us. How can we know if You have heard us?

In order to understand what we are saying, and with Whom we are speaking, we must recollect our outward senses, take charge of them ourselves and give them something that will occupy them. It is in this way that we have Heaven within ourselves since the Lord of Heaven is there. Once we get used to not raising our voices in order to speak to Him, since our Lord will make us conscious that He is there, we will be able to say the Paternoster and whatever other prayers we like with great peace of mind. The Lord Himself will help us not to grow tired. After we force ourselves to stay near the Lord, He will let us know that He heard our first Paternoster, even though we have had to say it many times. He loves to save us worry. So, if we can realize that we are with Him, what we are asking Him, how willing He is to grant it to us, how He loves to be with us and comfort us, we will understand that He has no wish for us to tire our brains by talking a great deal.

For the love of the Lord, then, get used to saying the Paternoster in this recollected way. You will soon see how much you gain by doing this. This is a method of prayer which establishes habits that prevent the soul from going astray and the faculties from becoming restless. You will discover this in time. Before long, you will have the great comfort of finding it unnecessary to tire yourselves with seeking this holy Father to Whom you pray, for you will discover Him within you.

May the Lord teach this to those of you who do not know it. I must confess that, until the Lord taught me this method, I never knew what it was to get satisfaction and comfort out of prayer. I have written about this custom of inner recollection at such length because I have gained so much from it.

Do not grow tired by trying to get used to this method. Gradually you will gain mastery over yourself, and your work is not in vain. To conquer yourself for your own good is to make use of the senses to serve the interior life. If you are praying, you must remember that there is One within you to Whom you can pray; if you are listening, you can listen to Him Who is nearer to you than anyone else. If you like, you never need to withdraw from this good companionship. You grieve when you have left your Father alone for so long even though you need Him so much.

If you can, you can practice recollection many times a day. If you cannot, you can do so occasionally. As you get used to it, you will feel its benefits sooner or later. Once the Lord has granted it to you, you will not trade it for any treasure.

If you practice this method of prayer for a year, you will be successful in attaining it, with God's help. This is such a short time for achieving such a solid foundation. If the Lord desires to raise you up to achieve great things, He will find you are ready because you will be close to Him. May Our Lord never allow us to withdraw ourselves from His presence.

CHAPTER

30

We must now think about the next petition in our good Master's prayer, in which He begins to entreat His holy Father on our behalf. We need to see for what He asks, since we should know this.

Who would not spend time thinking how to approach someone of importance so as to please the person and not to appear tedious? She would also think about what she was going to ask for and how she was going to use it, especially if her request was for something specific, as our good Jesus tells us our requests should be. Couldn't You, my Lord, have ended this prayer in a single sentence, saying: "Give us, Father, whatever is good for us"? In addressing One Who knows everything, there would seem to be no need to say anymore.

Eternal Wisdom, this would have been sufficient if it had been between You and Your Father. This is how You addressed Him in the Garden, telling Him Your will and Your fear, but leaving Yourself in His hands. You know us, my Lord, and You know that we are not as resigned as You were to Your Father's will. We need to be taught to ask for particular things so that we should stop for a moment to consider if what we ask of You is good for us. If it is not, we should not ask for it. But, because of our natures and having our free will, we will not accept what the Lord gives us if we do not receive what we ask for. The gift might be the best possible one, but we never think we are rich unless we actually see money in our hands.

What is it that sends our faith to sleep so that we cannot realize how certain we are to be punished and to be rewarded? It is good for you to know what you are asking for in the Paternoster. Thus, if the Eternal Father gives it to you, you will not throw it back in His face. You need to think carefully about what you ask for and whether it will be good for you. If it will not, do not ask for it. Instead, ask our Lord to give you light. We are blind and often have such an abhorrence of life-giving food that we cannot eat it but prefer what will cause us terrible and eternal death.

Now the good Jesus invites us to say these words, in which we pray that this Kingdom may come in us: "Hallowed be Your Name, Your Kingdom come in us." Think about how great our Master's wisdom is. Knowing of how little we are capable, our Lord saw that unless He provided for us by giving us His Kingdom here on earth, we could neither praise nor glorify the holy name of the Eternal Father in a fitting way. The good Jesus, therefore, places these two petitions side by side. We need to understand the importance of this thing we are praying for and pray for it without stopping and do all we can to please Him Who will give it to us.

Of the many joys to be found in the kingdom of Heaven, the greatest is that we will have no more to do with earthly things. In Heaven we will have an intrinsic tranquility and glory, a joy in the rejoicings of all, a perpetual peace, and a great interior satisfaction that we will have when we see we are praising the Lord and blessing His name. All there love Him, and the soul's one concern is loving Him. It cannot stop loving Him because it knows Him. This is how we should love Him on earth, though we cannot do so with the same perfection or all the time. If we knew Him, we would love Him very differently than we do now.

It looks like I am saying that we must be angels to make this petition and to say our vocal prayers well. Our Divine Master would like this, since He invites us to make so sublime a petition. You may be quite sure that He never tells us to ask for the impossible. With God's help, it must be possible for a soul living in that state of exile to reach such a point, though not as perfectly as those who have been freed from this prison. For we are making a sea voyage and are still on the journey. There are times, though, when we are tired of traveling. The Lord gives tranquility to our faculties and quiet to our souls. While they are quiet He gives us a clear understanding of the nature of the gifts He bestows on those whom He brings into His Kingdom. Those to whom on earth He grants requests receive pledges that give them great hope of attaining a perpetual enjoyment of what on earth He only allows them to taste.

Some might object that I am examining here pure contemplation, which is also called the Prayer of Quiet. But I am discussing vocal prayer here. I know there are many people who practice vocal prayer in the manner I have described and are raised by God to the higher kind of contemplation not through their own efforts.

Thus, it is important to say well your vocal prayers. I know a nun who could practice only vocal prayers. She kept up this practice and found she had everything else. If she omitted saying her prayers, her mind wandered so much that she could not endure it. We should all practice mental prayer like that. The number of Paternosters she said corresponded to the number of times our Lord shed His blood. She would spend her several hours of prayer on these and a few other prayers. She came to me once in great distress, saying that she did not know how to practice mental prayer, and that she could not contemplate but only say vocal prayers. I asked her what prayers she said, and from her reply I saw that she was experiencing pure contemplation and that the Lord was raising her to be in union with Him. She spent her life so well that her actions made it clear that she was receiving great favors. I praised the Lord and envied her vocal prayer. Any of you who have a bad opinion of contemplatives cannot think that you will be free from the risk of becoming like them if you keep a pure conscience and say your vocal prayers as they should be said.

CHAPTER

31

I still want to describe this Prayer of Quiet to you. It is in this kind of prayer that the Lord begins to show us that He is hearing our requests. He begins to give us His Kingdom on earth so that we may truly praise Him and strive to make others do the same.

This is a supernatural state, and no matter how hard we try, we cannot reach it ourselves. It is a state in which the soul enters into peace, or rather in which the Lord gives it peace through His presence, as He did to that just man Simeon. All the faculties are stilled in this state. The soul realizes that it is now very close to God, and that, if it were just a little bit closer, it would become one with Him. This is not because it sees Him either with its bodily or its spiritual eyes. The just man Simeon saw no more than the glorious Infant, a poor little Child Who might well have been the son of poor people rather than the Son of His Heavenly Father. The Child Himself revealed Who He was to Simeon. In the same way, though less clearly, the soul knows Who He is. It cannot understand how it knows Him, but it sees that it is in the Kingdom, and it feels such rev-

erence it does not dare ask anything. It is as if the
inward and outward body had fainted so that the
outward body does not want to move. It rests, like
one who has almost reached the end of her journey,
so it may have more strength to start on its way.

The body experiences the greatest delight, and the
soul is conscious of a deep satisfaction. It is so glad
to find itself near the fountain that it is full even
before it has begun to drink. There seems nothing
left for it to desire. The faculties are stilled and have
no desire to move, for any movement they make
appears to prevent the soul from loving God. They
are not completely lost, though, since, two of them
being free, they can realize Whose Presence they are
in. The will is in captivity now. If it is capable of
experiencing any pain in this state, the pain comes
when it realizes it will have to resume its freedom.
The mind tries to occupy itself with only one thing,
and the memory has no desire to occupy itself with
any more. They both see that this is the one necessary thing and that anything else will unsettle them.
People in this state prefer the body to remain
motionless, for otherwise their peace would be
destroyed. For this reason they do not dare to stir.
Speaking distresses them; they will spend an entire
hour on a single repetition of the Paternoster. They
are so close to God that they know they can make
themselves understood by signs. They are in the
palace, near to the King, and they see that He is
already beginning to give them His Kingdom on

earth. Sometimes they cry, but very gently and without worry. Their entire desire is to praise His name. They seem not to be in the world, and they have no wish to see or hear anything but their God. Nothing worries them, and it does not seem that anything ever can worry them. As long as they are in this state, they are so overwhelmed and absorbed by joy and delight that they do not wish for anything else.

Sometimes during this Prayer of Quiet, God grants the soul another favor which is hard to understand if one has not experienced it. Any of you who have had this experience will certainly recognize it, and it will comfort you to know what it is. I believe God often grants this favor with the other. When this quiet lasts for a long time, the peace cannot last for a long time if the will does not hold on to something. Sometimes this state lasts for two days, and we are full of joy even though we do not understand the reason for it. We see clearly that our entire self is not in what we are doing. The most important faculty—the will, which is united with God—is absent, and the other faculties are left free to involve themselves in His service. They have a great capacity for this service during this state, though these faculties are dull and stupid when attending to worldly affairs.

The Lord grants a great favor to these souls, for in them the active life is united with the contemplative. At such times they serve the Lord in both ways at once. The will, while in contemplation, is working without knowing how it does so. The other faculties are serving Him as Martha did. Thus Martha and Mary work together. I know someone whom the Lord often granted this experience. Although she could not understand it, a great contemplative assured her that it was indeed possible. I think that as the soul experiences such satisfaction in this Prayer of Quiet the will must be almost continuously united with Him Who alone can give it happiness.

I will give some advice here to those whom the Lord, out of His goodness alone, has brought to this state. When such people experience this joy, without knowing its source, they are tempted to imagine that they can prolong it and they may even try not to breathe. We can no more control this prayer than we can make the day break or stop night from falling. It is supernatural and something we cannot acquire. The most we can do to prolong this state is to realize that we can neither diminish nor add to it, but, being unworthy of it, we can receive it with great thanks. We can best give thanks, not with many words, but by lifting up our eyes.

We should seek greater solitude to make room for the Lord and allow Him to do His work in us. The most we should do is occasionally speak a single word, like a person giving a little puff to a candle that has almost gone out in order to make it burn again. If we begin to overwork our brains by making up long speeches, however, the will might again become active.

You will often find that these other two faculties do not help you at all. The soul may be enjoying the highest degree of quiet. The understanding may have soared so far aloft that it seems to be a guest in someone else's house, looking for other lodgings since it is not satisfied with its own house. At other times the mind seems to be settled in its own house and living there with the will as its companion. It is wonderful when all three faculties work together. The harmony is like that between husband and wife. If they are happy and love each other, both desire the same thing. If the husband is unhappy, he soon begins to make the wife restless. When the will finds itself in this state of quiet, it must ignore the understanding. For, if it tries to draw the understanding along with it, it is bound to grow restless. The result will be that the state of prayer will require great effort and the soul will lose what God has been giving it without any of its own effort.

The soul is like an infant still at its mother's breast. The mother cares so much for the infant that she gives it milk without its having to ask for it. This is what happens here. The will simply loves, and the understanding needs to make no effort. It is the Lord's pleasure that the soul should realize it is in His company, and should drink the sweet milk that the Lord puts into its mouth. The Lord wants the soul to know that it is He Who is granting this favor and that He too rejoices in the soul's enjoyment of it. It is not His will that the soul should try to understand how it is enjoying it or what it is enjoying. It should lose all thought of itself, and He Who is at its side will not fail to do what is best for it. If the soul begins to struggle with the mind, the soul will lose the milk and that Divine sustenance.

This state of prayer is different from that in which the soul is wholly united with God. In the latter state it does not even swallow its nourishment. The Lord simply gives this sustenance to the soul and the soul does not know the source of its nourishment. Even in this state, though, it seems that it is His will that the soul should work a little. What disturbs the soul is the understanding. This does not happen when all three faculties are united. He keeps them occupied with the enjoyment that He has given them, without their knowing, or being able to understand, the reason.

The soul is conscious of having reached this state of prayer—a quiet, deep, and peaceful happiness of the will, without being able to decide exactly what it is, though it does clearly see how it differs from the happiness of the world. To have dominion over the world would not bring the soul such inward satisfaction as it enjoys in the depths of its will. Other kinds of happiness in life touch only the outward part of the will.

When you find yourself in this state of prayer and the understanding wanders off in search of the most ridiculous things in the world, you should laugh at it and treat it like the silly thing it is. Stay in your state of quiet. Your thoughts will come and go, but the will is an all-powerful mistress and will recall them without your having to worry about it. If you try to drag the understanding back by force, you lose your power over it, which comes from the Divine sustenance, and both the will and the understanding will be losers. If we try hard to grasp everything, we lose everything. Experience will prove this to you.

When the soul achieves this state of prayer, it would seem that the Eternal Father has already granted its request that He will give it His Kingdom on earth. O blessed request, in which we ask for so great a good without knowing what we do. For this reason, we should be careful how we say the Paternoster, and all other vocal prayers and what we ask for in them. When God has shown us this favor, we will have to forget worldly things, all of which the Lord of the world has come and thrown out. Not everyone who experiences the Prayer of Quiet must be detached from the world. They must become more and more detached from everything, for otherwise they will remain where they are. If God gives a soul such pledges, it is a sign that He has great things in store for it. It will be her own fault if she does not make great progress. If He sees that the soul returns to earth after He has brought the Kingdom of Heaven into its house, the Lord will refrain from showing the soul the secrets of his Kingdom.

I think this is why there are not more spiritual

people in the world. They do not respond to so great a favor in a practical way. Instead of preparing themselves to receive more, they take back from the Lord the will that He considered His own and focus on worldly things. So, He seeks out others who love Him in order to grant them His greater gifts, although He will not take away all that He has given from those who live in purity of conscience. There are people—and I am one of them—to whom the Lord gives tenderness of devotion and holy inspirations and light on everything. He bestows this Kingdom on them and brings them to this Prayer of Quiet. Yet, they close their ears to His voice. They are so fond of repeating a large number of vocal prayers in a great hurry, as though they were anxious to finish their daily tasks, that when the Lord puts His Kingdom into their hands they do not accept it. They think they will be better off by reciting their prayers, which only distract them from their purpose.

Be careful when the Lord grants you this favor. Think about what a great treasure you may be losing. You need to realize that by repeating a single petition of the Paternoster you are doing much more than by repeating it in its entirety many times in a hurry and not thinking about what you are saying. He to Whom you are praying is very near, and He will not fail to hear you. You may be sure that you are truly praising Him and blessing His name, since you are glorifying the Lord as a member of His household and praising Him with increasing affection and desire so that you can never forsake His service.

O ur good Master has asked on our behalf, and has taught us to ask for a thing so precious that it includes all we can desire on earth. He has granted us the great gift of making us His brothers. Let us see what He wants us to give to His Father, and what He offers Him on our behalf. Let us see what He asks of us, for it is right that we should perform some great service for Him in return for such great gifts. What we give is in itself nothing at all by comparison with all that has been given us and with the greatness of Our Lord. My Lord, You leave us with something to give. We give all that we can if we give in the spirit of these words: "Your will be done, on earth as it is in Heaven."

You did well, O Lord, to make this last petition, so that we can accomplish what You promise in our name. For truly, Lord, if You had not done this, I do not think we could have accomplished it. Since Your Father does what You ask in granting us His Kingdom on earth, I know we can truly fulfill Your word by giving what You promise in our name. For since my earth has now become Heaven, it will be possible for Your will to be done in me. On an earth so wretched and barren as mine, Lord, I do not know how it could be possible in any other way. You offer a great thing.

When I think about this, it amuses me that there are people who say that we should not ask the Lord for trials because it shows little humility. I have found some people so weak that, even without making this pretext of humility, they do not have the courage to pray for trials, because they think that these would be given to them at once. I should like to ask them what they understand this to mean which they ask our Lord to fulfill in them. Do they say this because everyone else says it and not because they want it to be done? That would not be right. Remember that the good Jesus is our Ambassador here, and that His desire has been to mediate between us and His Father at a great cost to Himself. It would not be right for us to refuse to give what He promises and offers on our behalf. Whether we want it or not, God's will must be done in both Heaven and on earth. Do as I suggest, then, and make a virtue of necessity.

I find it a great comfort that You did not trust the fulfillment of Your will to one as wretched as I. Blessed be You forever and let all things praise You. May Your name be glorified forever. I would have had to be very good indeed to hold the fulfillment of Your will in Heaven and on earth in my hands. Though my will is not yet free from self-interest, I give it freely to You. By experience I have learned how much I gain by leaving it freely in Your hands. We lose a great deal by not fulfilling our promises to the Lord in the Paternoster and giving Him what we offer Him.

I will explain to you how much you are offering. Do not behave like some religious people, who do nothing but promise and then excuse themselves for not fulfilling their promises by saying they did not understand what they were promising. It seems very easy to say that we will surrender our will to someone, until we try it and realize that it is the hardest thing we can do if we carry it out as we should. The Lord knows what each of us can bear. When He sees that one of us is strong, He does not hesitate to fulfill His will in her.

I want you to realize with Whom you are dealing and what the good Jesus offers on your behalf to the Father. I want you to realize what you are giving Him when you pray that His will may be done in you. We are praying for nothing else. Do not fear that He will give you riches or pleasures or great honors or any such earthly things. His love for you is not so poor as that. He places a very high value on what you give Him and wants to repay you for it since He gives you His Kingdom while you are still alive. Would you like to see how He treats those who make this prayer from their hearts? Ask His glorious Son, Who asked this prayer in the Garden. Think about His determination and the fullness of

His desire as He prayed. Think whether or not God's will was perfectly fulfilled in Him through the trials, sufferings, insults, and persecutions He gave Him, until His life ended with death on a Cross.

You can see what God gave to His best Beloved and you can understand from that what His will is. These are His gifts in this world. He gives them in proportion to the love He has for us. He gives more to those He loves most, and less to those He loves least. He gives according to the courage each of us has and the love we bear to our Lord. When He sees a soul who loves Him greatly, He knows that soul can suffer much for Him, whereas one who loves Him little will suffer little. I believe that love is the measure of our ability to bear crosses, whether great or small. If you have this love, do not let your prayers be words of mere politeness. Be prepared to suffer what our Lord desires. If you give Him your will in any other way, you are just showing Him a jewel and asking Him to take it and then pulling it away when He puts out His hand to take it.

Such mockery is no way to treat One who endured so much for us. If for no other reason than this, it would not be right to mock Him so often, for we say these words often to Him in the Paternoster. Let us give Him the jewel that we have so often tried to give Him. For the truth is that He gives it to us first so that we may give it back to Him. Worldly people will do a great deal if they sincerely resolve to fulfill the will of God. Religious people must both say and act, and give him both words and deeds. Yet, we sometimes try to give God the jewel but we even put it into His hand and then take it back again. We are so generous all of a sudden, and then we become so mean that it would have been better if we had stopped to think before giving.

The aim of all my advice to you in this book is that we should surrender ourselves entirely to the Creator, place our will in His hands, and detach ourselves from the creatures. I will tell you why our good Master puts these words here. He knows how much we will gain by performing this service for His Eternal Father. We are preparing ourselves for the time, which will come very soon, when we will find ourselves at the end of our journey and will be drinking living water from the fountain. Unless we surrender our will totally to the Lord and place ourselves in His hands so He may do what is best for us in accordance with His will, He will never allow us to drink from it. This is the perfect contemplation about which you asked me to write.

We cannot do anything ourselves in this matter, either through hard work or by thorough planning, and we don't need to do so anyway. Everything else prevents us from saying: "Your will be done"; that is, may the Lord fulfill His will in me in every way that He desires. If You will do this by means of trials, give me strength and let the trials come to me. If You are going to give me sickness and need, I will not turn my face away from You, and I do not have the right to turn my back on sickness and poverty. For Your Son gave You my will in the name of us all and it is not right that I should fail. Grant me the grace of bestowing on me Your Kingdom so I may do Your will, since He has asked me to do this. Treat me as one of Your own, according to Your will.

What a powerful gift this is. If it is made with proper determination, it will draw the Almighty to become one with our lowly natures, transform us into Himself, and to bring about a union between the Creator and the creature. What a rich reward this is for you from the hands of such a good Master. Knowing how to gain His Father's good will, He teaches us how to serve Him.

The more determined we are and the more we show Him by our actions that our words to Him are not mere nonsense, the more Our Lord draws us to Himself and raises us above all petty earthly things. He raises us up so that we may receive great gifts from Him. His rewards for our service do not end with this life. He values our service so much that we do not know what else we can ask for. Our Lord never gets tired of giving. He is not content with having united this soul with Himself. He begins to cherish it, to reveal secrets to it, to rejoice in its understanding of what it has gained and in the knowledge it has of all He has yet to give it. He causes it gradually to lose its exterior senses so that nothing may occupy it. This we call rapture. He makes such a friend of the soul that not only does

He restore its will to it but He gives it His own. He is making a friend of it, and He is glad to allow it to rule with Him. He does what the soul asks of Him, just as the soul does what He commands. He is all-powerful and can do whatever He desires, and His desire never comes to an end.

Despite its desires, the poor soul is often unable to do all it would like. It cannot do anything unless it is given power. It grows richer and richer. The more it serves, the greater its debt becomes. It often grows tired of being subjected to the inconveniences it has to endure while it is imprisoned in the body. It would gladly resolve its debts, for it is quite tired. Even if we do all that is in us, however, how can we repay God? We have nothing to give except what we first received. We can only learn to know ourselves and do what we can, namely, surrender our will and fulfill God's will in us. I have described the nature of this prayer in other places. I have also described the way that the soul should behave at such a time. Since I have said a great deal about what the soul feels and how it knows this to be the work of God, I do no more than touch here on the life of prayer in order to show you how to repeat this prayer, the Paternoster.

Do not suppose that you can reach this state by your own effort or diligence. You must practice simplicity and humility, for those are the virtues that achieve everything. You must say: "Your will be done."

CHAPTER
33

The good Jesus understands that He is offering a difficult thing on our behalf. He knows our weakness. We often show that we do not understand what the Lord's will is, since we are so weak while He is so merciful. He knows that we must find some way not to neglect to give what He has given on our behalf. If we did neglect this, it would not be good for us, since everything we gain comes from what we give. He knows it will be hard for us to carry this out. If anyone were to tell a wealthy person that it is God's will that he should eat more moderately so that others dying of hunger would at least have bread to eat, he will find a thousand reasons for not understanding this but interpreting it his own way. If one tells a person who speaks badly of others that it is God's will to love his neighbor as himself, he will lose patience, and no amount of reasoning will convince him. If one tells a religious that it is God's will that he should fulfill his vows and not cause a scandal by acting contrary to them, some religious would still want their own way. What would be the case, then, if the Lord had not already done most of what was necessary in His remedy to us? Very few would be able to fulfill the petition: "Your will be done." Realizing our need, the good Jesus has shown us the extreme love that He has for us. In His own name and in that of his brothers He has made this petition: "Give us, Lord, this day our daily bread."

Let us realize the meaning of our good Master's petition. Don't set much store by what you have given, since you will receive so much. The good Jesus knew what He had given for us and how important it was for us to give this to God. He knew it would be difficult for us because of our natural inclination to weakness and our lack of love and courage. He saw that we need Him to aid us not just once but every day. This is why He was determined to stay with us. He wanted it to come from the Eternal Father's hand. Father and the Son are one and the same, and He knew that whatever He did on earth God would do in Heaven. Since His will and the Father's will were one, the Son knew God would consider good whatever He did. Even so, He wanted to ask His Father's permission, for He knew that He was His beloved Son and that God was well pleased with Him. He knew that in this petition He was asking for more than He had asked for in the others, but He already knew what death He was to suffer and what dishonor and insults He would have to bear.

What father could there be, Lord, who, after giving us his son would allow him to remain among us day after day to suffer so much? None, Lord, but Yours. You know well of Whom You are asking this. The Son's love is so great and the Father's love is so great. I am not so amazed at the good Jesus, since He has already said, "Your will be done." Being Who He is, He was bound to put His words into practice. He is not like us. Knowing that He was carrying out His words by loving us as He loves Himself, He sought ways He could carry out this commandment more perfectly, even at His own cost. How, Eternal Father, could You consent to this? How can You see Your Son every day in such wicked hands? Ever since You permitted Your Son to become human, You see how He has been treated. How can Your Mercy see Him insulted every day? How many insults are being offered today to this Most Holy Sacrament? How often must the Father see Him in the hands of His enemies? What blasphemies these heretics commit.

Eternal Lord, how can You grant such a petition? How can You consent to it? Think of His love, which allows Him to submit to being cut to pieces daily for the sake of fulfilling Your will and helping us. You see this, Lord, for Your Son does not allow any obstacle to stand in His way. Why must all the blessings we receive be at His cost? How is it that He is silent in the face of everything and speaks not for Himself but only for us? Is there anyone who will speak for this most loving Lamb? Give me permission to speak for Him, Lord, since You have left Him in our power.

Let me address You on His behalf, since He gave You such full obedience and surrendered Himself to us with such great love.

I have been thinking how in this petition alone the same words are repeated. First, the Lord speaks of "our daily bread" and asks You to give it to us. Then He says, "Give it to us today, Lord." He puts the matter to His Father in this way. The Father gave us His Son once and for all to die for us. Thus, He is our own. He does not want the gift to be taken from us until the end of the world, but He leaves it to us to help us every day. This should melt your hearts, for there is no slave who would willingly call himself by that name. The good Jesus considers it an honor, however.

Eternal Father, how great is the value of this humility. With what a treasure we are purchasing Your Son. We already know how to sell Him, for He was sold for thirty pieces of silver. But what price is sufficient to purchase Him? Since He is made one with us through that part of our nature which is His, and being Lord of His own will, He reminds His Father that, since our nature is His, He is able to give it to us and to say "our bread." He does not differentiate Himself from us, though we differentiate ourselves from Him by not giving ourselves daily for Our Lord's sake.

34

We have come to the conclusion that the good Jesus, being ours, asks His Father to let us have Him daily, which means forever. I have been pondering why the Lord says, "Give us this day, Lord" after He says "our daily bread." It seems to me that this bread is ours daily because we have Him here on earth, since He has remained with us here and we receive Him. If we gain from His company, we will also have Him in Heaven. The only reason He remains with us is to help and encourage and sustain us so we will do that which is to be fulfilled in us.

In saying "this day" He seems to be thinking of a day of the length of this life. For the poor souls who will bring damnation upon themselves and will not experience Him in the world to come, they are His own creatures. He did everything to help them and was with them to strengthen them throughout the "today" of this life. It is not His fault that they are overcome. They will not have an excuse and they will not be able to complain that the Father took His bread from them at a time when they needed it the most. Thus, the Son always prays to the Father that, since this life lasts no more than a day, He will allow Him to spend it in our service. Since God has already given us His Son by sending Him of His will alone into this world, so He does not care to abandon us. He remains here with us for the greater glory of His friends and for the discomfort of His enemies. He prays for nothing more than this "today" since He has given us this most holy Bread. He has given us this sustenance and manna of humanity forever. We can have it whenever we want it, and if we die of hunger it will be our own fault. In whatever ways the soul desires to partake of food, it will find joy and comfort in the Most Holy Sacrament. There is no trial or persecution that we cannot bear easily if we partake and taste those trials that He Himself bore.

We should not always remind the Lord about the bread that sustains our physical bodies nor should we be concerned about it. Stay on the level of highest contemplation. If we remain on such a level, we will not remember that we are in the world, and we will certainly not be concerned with food. Would the Lord ever have insisted on our asking for food, or taught us to do so by His own example? No, He teaches us to fix our desires on heavenly things and to pray that we can begin to enjoy these while here on earth. He knew that once we began to worry about the needs of the body, we would forget the needs of the soul. Besides, should we be satisfied with just a little and thus pray for a little? The more food we are given, the less we get of the water from Heaven.

Ask the Lord to let you have your Spouse today so that as long as you live you will never find yourself in this world without Him. Once you realize that He remains disguised beneath these accidents of bread and wine, this will strengthen your joy. His concealment is a real torture to those who have no other love or consolation. Ask Him to prepare you to receive Him worthily.

If you have truly abandoned yourself to God's will, you will not be anxious about the bread of the body. In these hours of prayer you are dealing with more important matters. There will be enough time to work and earn your daily bread. Try not to let your thoughts dwell on this. Work with your body, for you must try to support yourselves. But let your soul be at rest. Leave such anxiety about earthly things to your Spouse, and He will always bear it for you. He will not fail you if you keep your promises and abandon yourself to God's will.

If you have really surrendered yourselves to God, stop being anxious for yourselves, for He will always bear your anxiety. It is like a servant who is anxious to please his master in everything. The master is bound to provide food for the servant as long as he stays in the master's house and works for him. Would it be right for the servant to go every day to the master and ask him for food when he knew his master would take care of him? He would be wasting his words. His master would tell him to mind his business of serving. If the servant worried unnecessarily he would not perform his work as well as he could. Some of you may worry about earthly bread. Let us pray to our Eternal Father that we deserve our heavenly bread. Although we cannot feast our bodily eyes on Him since He is hidden from us, He may reveal Himself to the eyes of the soul and make Himself known to us as another kind of delightful food that sustains our life.

Don't you think that this most holy food provides ample sustenance for the body as well as a potent medicine for bodily sickness? I know a person who had serious illnesses and often suffered great pain. This pain was taken away from her in a flash and she became quite well again. Such things happen quite often. There is no need to speak of the many other effects produced in this soul. This person had such devotion that when she heard people say they wished to live in Christ's time, she smiled to herself. She knew that He is here with us in the Most Holy Sacrament just as He was here then, and she wonders what more they could possibly want.

This same person, who was by no means perfect, always tried to strengthen her faith. When she prayed she thought she saw Him with her own bodily eyes entering her house. She truly believed that the Lord was entering her poor house, and she stopped thinking about outward things and went into her house with Him. She tried to recollect her senses so that they might all become aware of this great blessing and so that they would not keep the soul from becoming conscious of it. She imagined herself at His feet and wept with the Magdalen exactly as if she had seen Him with her bodily eyes in the Pharisee's house. Even if she felt no devotion, faith told her it was good for her to be there.

For, unless we want to be blind and foolish, and if we have faith, it is clear that He is within us. Why, then, do we need to go and seek Him a long way off? We know that the good Jesus is with us until we have consumed the accidents of bread with our natural energy. How can we doubt that He will work miracles when He is within us, if we have faith? How can we doubt that He will give us what we ask of Him since He is in our house?

If you are unhappy that you cannot see Him with your bodily eyes, remember that it would not be good for us. It is one thing to see Him glorified and quite another to see Him as He was when He lived in this world. Our weak natures could not endure the sight anyway. Having once seen the Eternal Truth, people would realize that all the things we hold dear on this earth are false. If we could see such great Majesty, how could miserable sinners remain so close to Him after having offended Him so greatly? We can approach Him beneath the Bread. If the King disguises Himself, we don't need to be concerned about coming to Him so cautiously. By disguising Himself, He has obliged Himself to submit to this. Otherwise, who would dare approach Him with so many imperfections and with such lukewarm zeal?

We do not know what we ask. His Wisdom knows better than we what we need. He reveals Himself to those He knows will gain from His presence. Though unseen by bodily eyes, He has many ways of revealing Himself to the soul through deep inward emotions. Be happy to remain with Him. The hour after Communion is an excellent time for talking with Him; do not squander it. If it is your responsibility to perform some other task, try to leave your soul with the Lord. He is your Master, and He will not fail to teach you. But if you start thinking about other things and do not pay any more attention to Him, and do not care that He is within you, He cannot reveal Himself to you. This hour after Communion is a good time for our Master to teach us and for us to listen to Him. While you say the Paternoster, you should realize that you are in the company of the one Who taught it to you. Kiss His feet in thanks for His teaching you, and ask Him to show you how to pray and never to leave you.

You may be in the habit of praying while looking at a picture of Christ. It seems foolish to me to turn away from the Person Himself to look at His picture. Wouldn't it be foolish if we had a portrait of a loved one and we carried on our conversation with the portrait whenever this person came to visit? I find it helpful to use a picture only when the person is absent. Then we can take great comfort in looking at the picture of Him Whom we have such reason to love. This is a great inspiration and makes us wish we could see the picture wherever we turned our eyes. What can we look upon that is better or more attractive to the sight than upon Him Who so dearly loves us and contains within Himself all good things?

When you have received the Lord and are in His presence, try to shut your bodily eyes and to open your soul's eyes and look into your own hearts. Practice this habit of staying with Him whenever you pray. Strive to keep your conscience clear so that you can rejoice in your Good. He will not disguise Himself that you will not be able to know His presence. He will make Himself known to you according to the desire you have to see Him. Your longing for Him may be so great that He will reveal Himself to you wholly.

If we pay attention to Him only when we have received Him and go away in search of other earthly things, what can He do? Will He have to drag us forcefully to look at Him because He desires to reveal Himself to us? When He revealed Himself to all people plainly, they did not treat Him well at all, and very few of them even believed Him. So, He grants us a great blessing when He shows us that it is He Who is in the Most Holy Sacrament. He will not reveal Himself openly or communicate His glories except to those who greatly want Him, for they are His true friends. Anyone who is not a true friend and does not receive God as a true friend, after doing all in her power to prepare for Him, must never urge Him to reveal Himself to her. The hour is hardly even over when such a person, who has spent time fulfilling the Church's commandment, goes home and tries to drive Christ out of the house. Being occupied with business and worldly things, she seems to be hurrying to prevent the Lord from taking possession of His own house.

CHAPTER
35

Entering into solitude with God is extremely important. You will gain a great deal by communicating spiritually while you are hearing the Mass. If you practice inward recollection in the same fashion after the Mass, you learn how to love the Lord deeply. If we prepare to receive Him, He never fails to give, and He gives in many ways we cannot understand. It is like approaching a fire. The fire might be a large one, but if we stayed a long way from it and covered our hands, the fire would not warm us very much, even though we would be warmer than if we were in a place where we had no fire at all. There is a difference when we try to approach the Lord, though. If the soul is properly prepared, and comes with the intention of driving out the cold, it will retain its warmth for hours. If any spark flies out, it will set it on fire.

If at first He does not reveal Himself to you and you do not grasp this practice, the devil will make you think that you can find more devotion in other things and less devotion in this practice. But do not give up this method, for the Lord will use it to prove your love for Him. There are few souls who remain with Him and follow Him in His trials. If we endure something for our Lord, He will repay us. There are also irreverent people who not only wish not to be with Him but who insult Him and drive Him from their homes. We must endure trials, then, to show Him that we have the desire to see Him. He is treated badly and neglected in many places. But He suffers everything if He finds one soul that will receive Him with love as its Guest. Let this be your soul. If there were no such souls, the Eternal Father would refuse to allow Him to remain with us. God is so good a Friend to those who are His friends, and so good a Master to those who are His servants, that He will not keep the Son from so excellent a work when He knows it is His Beloved Son's will. In this work His Son reveals fully the love that He has for His Father.

There must be someone, Holy Father, who will speak for Your Son, for He has never defended Himself. Even though this seems presumptuous, let us perform this task. We must rely, though, on our Lord's command to us to pray to Him. Let us ask our Lord, in the name of the good Jesus, that, since the Son has done everything He could do to give mercy to sinners, He keep the Son from being treated so badly. Since His Holy Son has provided this way that we can offer Him frequently as a sacrifice, let us use this precious gift to stop the evil and irreverence which many Christians pay to this Most Holy

Sacrament. Many Christians go to church meaning to offend Him rather than to worship Him.

Why does this happen, my Lord and my God? Give us a solution for such grievous wrongs, which even our sinful hearts cannot endure. I ask You, Eternal Father, not to endure it any longer. Remember that Your Son is still in the world. With His purity and beauty He does not deserve to be in such a house where such things happen. Extinguish this fire, Lord, for Your Son's sake. We would not pray that He no longer remain with us, for You have granted His prayer to You to leave Him with us until the end of the world. What would happen to us if He were to go? Since You must remedy this situation in some way, Lord, I ask You to do so. You are able to do so, if You so will it.

I wish I could urge You persistently on this matter. If I had served You better, I might be able to ask You so great a favor as a reward for my services. You reward all services. But I have not served You, God. Perhaps my sins and my great offense to You have brought so many evils into the world. The only thing I can do, then, my Creator, is to give You this blessed Bread. I return it to You even though You gave it to us. Calm this sea, Lord, and take this ship, Your Church, out of this great tempest. Save us, my Lord, for we perish.

If we have this heavenly food, everything is easy
for us. We are able to show the Father that we
can do His will. He now asks God to forgive us
our debts as we ourselves forgive others. Continuing
the prayer that He is teaching us, He says: "Forgive
us, Lord, our debts, even as we forgive them to our
debtors."

He does not say: "as we will forgive." Anyone
who asks for such a gift as the one mentioned, and
has already yielded his will to God's will, must have
forgiven others already. So He says: "as we forgive
our debtors." Anyone who sincerely repeats the petition, "May Your will be done," must have already
forgiven others, at least in intention. You can see
now why the saints rejoiced in insults and persecutions; it gave them something to present to the Lord
when they prayed to Him. What can somebody like
me do? I have so little to forgive others and so much
to have forgiven. We need to consider this matter
carefully. Since God has pardoned our sins, which
deserve eternal fire, we must pardon all the little
things that people have done to us and which are not

wrongs at all. How is it possible to injure someone like me who deserves to be plagued eternally by devils? Isn't it right that I be plagued in this world, too? For this reason, then, my Lord, I have nothing to give You in begging You to forgive my debts. Your Son's pardon of me must be a free gift. Your Son must pardon me, for no one has done me any injustice. Thus, there is nothing that I can pardon for Your sake. I do have the desire to so forgive, Lord, for I believe I would forgive any wrong if You would forgive me and I might do Your will unconditionally. If I were condemned without cause, I do not know what I might do. You are Blessed, for You put up with one who is so poor. When Your most holy Son makes this petition in the name of all humankind, I cannot be included, for I have nothing to give.

What if there are other people like me who have not discovered the state they are in? I would ask them not to pay attention to the tiny slights they receive. If they insist on these nice points of honor, they are like children building houses of straw. If we really knew what honor is and what it means to lose it! I am speaking mainly about myself here. I was proud of my honor without knowing the meaning of honor. I just followed the examples of others. I used to feel slighted so easily. I never grasped the essence of the matter, though, because I never thought about true honor. Our souls gain a great deal by having true honor. The world teaches that we can profit by possessing the world's honor. But, the world's teaching is backward, for the soul does not gain anything by having worldly honor. Thank you, Lord, for taking us out of the world.

Taking honor and rank so seriously is enough to make one weep. We should do everything with humility and according to our religious principles. If we are too concerned about worldly honor, we will never rise as far as Heaven. We are attracted by the thought of rising higher, and we dislike climbing down. Aren't You our Example, O Lord and Master? In what did Your honor consist, O Lord, You Who have honored us? Did You lose it when You were humbled even to death? No, You gained it for all humankind.

We have lost our way because we have taken the wrong path from the very beginning. May God grant that no soul be lost through its attention to such vanity regarding honor, especially when it doesn't know what honor means. We will get to the point where we think we have done something wonderful because we have forgiven a person for some insignificant thing that was not an insult or a slight. Then we will ask the Lord to forgive us as people who have done something important, just because we have forgiven someone. Help us, Lord, to understand that we do not really know what we are saying. We have empty hands when we come to You to ask You to forgive us. Out of Your mercy, forgive us.

The Lord must value greatly this mutual love of ours for one another. Since we have given Him our wills, we have given Him complete rights over us, and we cannot do that without love. It is important for us to love one another and to be at peace. The good Jesus might have put everything else before our love for one another and said: "Forgive us, Lord, for we are doing a great deal of penance, praying often, or fasting, and because we have left all for Your sake and love You greatly." But He never said: "because we would lose our lives for Your sake," or any of these other things He might have said. He simply says: "because we forgive." Perhaps the reason He said this was because He knew that mutual love was the hardest virtue for us to reach, though it is the virtue dearest to His Father. Because of its great difficulty He put it where He did. After having asked for so many great gifts for us, He offers it on our behalf to God.

Note that He says: "as we forgive." Unless a person is very determined and makes a point of forgiving both these insignificant things and any serious evil, you need not think much of this person's prayer. Wickedness has no effect upon a soul whom God draws to Himself in such a sublime prayer as this one. This soul does not care whether it is highly esteemed or not. That is not quite correct, for honor is more distressing than dishonor, and the soul prefers trials to a great deal of rest and ease. Anyone to whom the Lord has given His Kingdom no longer wants a kingdom in this world. She knows she is going the right way to reign in a much more exalted manner, having already discovered by experience what great benefits the soul gains and what progress it makes when it suffers for God's sake. Our Lord grants such consolations very rarely, and then only to those who have willingly endured many trials for His sake. Contemplatives have to bear heavy trials, and thus the Lord seeks out for Himself souls of great experience.

These people have already learned how to value everything properly. They do not pay any attention to things that fade away with time. They may be upset momentarily by a great trial. They will hardly feel such trials when reason intervenes and drives away their distress by helping them to see how God has given them the opportunity of gaining in a single day more lasting favor in Our Lord's sight than they could gain in ten years by means of trials that they sought for themselves. This is not unusual. Contemplatives desire and treasure trials just as others desire and treasure jewels and money. Contemplatives know that trials will make them rich.

Contemplatives would never honor themselves unduly. They want their sins to be known, and they will talk about their sins to people who want to put the contemplatives in a place of high honor. The same is true of their genealogy, which they know will be of no use to them in the Eternal Kingdom. Coming from a good family would only be good if it helped them to serve God better. If they do not come from a good family, it upsets them when people think they are better than they are. The contemplatives are pleased to inform these people that they have not come from a good family. Those to whom God grants humility and such great love for Him forget themselves when they can perform greater services for Him. They cannot believe there are other people who are so concerned with the things that they do not consider to be wrongs.

As I have said, those who are united to God in perfect contemplation are the ones who experience these things. You can quickly see the determination to suffer wrongs, even though the suffering brings anguish, in anyone to whom the Lord has granted this grace of prayer and the grace of attaining union. If these experiences do not occur in a soul, and it is not strengthened by prayer, you will know that this was not Divine grace but indulgence and illusion coming from the devil to make us attach more importance to our honor.

When the Lord first grants these favors, the soul will not immediately attain this strength. If He continues to grant them, though, He will soon give the soul courage and strength, certainly with regard to forgiveness. I cannot believe that a soul that has come so near to Mercy Itself and has learned the greatness of God's pardon will not be immediately ready to forgive and remain on good terms with the person who has done it wrong. Such a soul remembers the consolation and grace that God has shown it. It has recognized the signs of great love, and it is happy for the opportunity to show Him love in return.

I know many people who have become contemplatives. Though I notice other faults in them, I have never seen such a person who was unforgiving. If you receive God's grace, look within yourself and be sure that it is making you into a forgiving person. If it is not, this grace does not come from God, Who always enriches the soul when He visits it. Although the grace and consolations may fade with time, the benefits of this grace endure. Since the good Jesus knows this well, He assures His Holy Father that we are forgiving our debtors.

We should give great praise to the Lord for the sublime perfection of this prayer. It was so well composed by the Master that each may use it in her own way. I am astounded when I think that in its few words are preserved all contemplation and perfection. If we study this prayer, we do not need any other books. Thus far in the Paternoster, the Lord has taught us the whole method of prayer and of high contemplation, from the very beginnings of mental prayer to Quiet and Union. Our Lord is here beginning to explain to us the effects this prayer produces.

I have often wondered why our Lord did not explain such sublime subjects in greater detail. I think that He meant this prayer to be a general one that could be used by all. Everyone could interpret it as she saw fit and ask for what she wanted and find comfort in doing so. Contemplatives, who no longer want earthly things, and people devoted to God, can ask for heavenly favors which, through God's great goodness, may be given to us on earth. Others, who must live by the rules of their state, may also ask for the bread they need for the sustenance and maintenance of their families. They may also ask for other things as they need them.

Blessed be His name for ever and ever. For His sake, I ask the Eternal Father to forgive my debts and grievous sins. Although no one has wronged me, and I do not have anyone to forgive, I myself need forgiveness every day. I pray that God will give me grace every day to make this prayer.

The good Jesus has taught us a sublime method of prayer and asked that, even in our exile, we may be like the angels if we try as hard as we can to make our actions match our words. We should be like the children of such a Father. Our Lord knows that if our actions and our words are one, the Lord will help without fail to fulfill our petitions, give us His kingdom, and help us through supernatural gifts, like the Prayer of Quiet and perfect contemplation. Everything we achieve by ourselves is of little consequence.

We must all surrender our will to God and forgive others. Some will practice these more and some less. Those who are perfect will surrender their wills and will forgive others with perfection. We will do what we can, and the Lord will accept it all. It is as if He were to make an agreement with His Eternal Father on our behalf and to say: "Do this, Lord, and My brethren will do that." He will not fail us. His rewards are limitless.

We should say this prayer in such a way that there is no doubt that we will do what we say. He will then reward us greatly. We must never be insincere with Him, for He loves us to be honest with Him, never saying one thing and meaning another. He will always, then, give us more than we ask for. Our good Master knows that those who attain real perfection in their petitions will reach this high degree through the Father's favors. Those who are already perfect or near perfection need not be afraid, for they say they have left the world behind, and the Lord is pleased with them. They will possess the greatest hope of our Lord's pleasure from the effects He produces in their souls. They are so absorbed in these joys that they want to forget there is any other world or that they have enemies.

How wonderful it is to have a wise and prudent Master who foresees our dangers. This is the greatest blessing that the spiritual soul still on earth can want, for it brings great security. The Lord needed to awaken these souls and remind them that they have enemies. If they are not to fall or be deceived, they need a great deal more help from the Eternal Father. So He makes these petitions: "And lead us not into temptation, but deliver us from evil."

CHAPTER 38

There are great things for us to meditate on and to learn to understand as we pray. It is quite certain that those who attain perfection do not ask the Lord to deliver them from trials or temptations. This is just a sign that this contemplation that the Lord gives them is not illusion but comes truly from the Spirit of the Lord. Perfect souls are not repelled by trials, but pray for them and love them. They are like soldiers; the more wars there are, the more pleased they are because they hope to emerge from the war with greater riches. If there are no wars, they serve for their pay, but they know that this pay will not make them rich.

The soldiers of Christ—those who experience contemplation and practice prayer—are always ready for the hour of conflict. They are never afraid of their open enemies, for they know who they are and know that the Lord will give them strength to fight. They will always be victorious and gain great riches. They rightly fear, though, the treacherous enemies, and they ask the Lord to deliver them from these enemies. Such enemies are devils who transform themselves and disguise themselves as the angels of light. The souls fail to recognize them until these enemies have done a great deal of harm. They put an end to our virtues, and we continue to yield to temptations without knowing it. Let us pray to the Lord often in the Paternoster to deliver us from these kinds of enemies. May He deliver us from temptations that deceive us. How rightly our good Master teaches us to pray for this deliverance.

Think about the many ways these enemies harm us. The sole danger does not lie in their making us believe, when they give us consolations, that these come from God. This is the least harmful thing they can do. It might even help persuade us to spend more time in prayer and to make greater progress. Not knowing that these consolations come from the devil, and knowing that they are unworthy of such gifts, they will never stop giving thanks to God and will feel a greater obligation to serve Him. They will strive to prepare themselves for more of God's favors, since they believe these come from His hand.

Always seek humility and realize you are unworthy of these graces and do not seek them. Our Lord regards our intention, which is to please Him, serve Him, and keep Him near in prayer. The Lord is faithful. Be careful not to let your humility break down into vanity. Ask the Lord to deliver you from this, and you don't need to be afraid that He will allow anyone but Himself to comfort you.

The devil can do great harm by making us believe

we possess virtues that we do not possess. When we receive God's grace, we feel we are doing nothing and have a greater obligation to serve. When the devil deceives us, though, we think we are giving and serving and that the Lord should reward us. Our humility is weakened and we neglect to cultivate it since we think we already have it. We think we are walking safely when, without realizing it, we stumble and fall into a pit from which we cannot escape. Though we may not consciously have committed any sin that would have sent us to hell, we have sprained our ankles and cannot continue on the road on which we have been traveling. No one at the bottom of a huge pit makes much progress. It will be her end, and she will be lucky if she does not fall right down to hell. At best, she will never be able to continue on her journey. A great many passersby also fall into this pit. Only if the person who has fallen in gets out and fills the pit with earth will she prevent further harm to herself and others. What can we do about this? The best thing seems to be to do what our Master teaches us: to pray and to ask the Eternal Father to deliver us from temptation.

If we think the Lord has given us a certain grace, we must also realize that He may take it away from us. Haven't you noticed this? Sometimes I think that I am extremely detached from worldly things, but other times I find I am so attached to things that I might have previously scorned. Sometimes I find that I have such great courage that I am not afraid of anything, but the following day I find I cannot kill an ant for God's sake even if someone challenged me not to do it. Sometimes people's words do not bother me, and other times I am so disturbed by their words that I want to leave the world altogether. Who can say, then, that she is rich if at the time when she most needs a certain virtue she finds she lacks it? Our treasure must come from somewhere else, and we never know when God will leave us in our prison of misery without giving us any. If others, thinking we are good, give us honor, they and we will look foolish when it becomes clear that these virtues have only been loaned to us. If we serve the Lord with humility, He will provide for our needs. If we are not humble, the Lord will leave us to ourselves. This is a great favor on His part, for He helps us to realize that we possess nothing that He has not given to us.

Sometimes the devil makes us believe we have some virtue because we are determined to suffer a great deal for God's sake. We really and truly believe we would suffer all this, and the devil encourages this belief, so we are pleased. Do not rely on these virtues. We do not know anything about such virtues until we are put to a test. Your patience might fail you the first time someone says an annoying word to you. If you have to suffer frequently, praise God for beginning to teach you this virtue. Force yourself to suffer patiently, for this is a sign that He wants you to repay Him for the virtue He is giving you.

The devil also tempts us to appear poor in spirit. Although we are in the habit of saying that we want nothing and care for nothing, our poverty of spirit disappears as soon as the chance comes that we may be given something, even though we do not need it in the least. When we say this over and over, we begin to think that we really are poor in spirit. We must always be careful and recognize this temptation. When the Lord gives one of these virtues, the rest come with it. Even if you think you possess this virtue, always be suspicious that you are mistaken. The truly humble person doubts her own virtues, for these virtues seem more genuine and worthier when she sees them in her neighbors.

We must also be very careful, for the devil instills in us a humility that makes us uneasy about the seriousness of our past sins. "Am I worthy to approach the Sacrament?" "Am I in a good disposition?" "I am not fit to live among good people." Things like these, when they come with tranquility, joy, and pleasure, and are suggested by our own knowledge of ourselves, should be highly honored. If they are accompanied by turmoil, unrest, and depression of the soul, and you cannot calm yourself, you may be sure it is a temptation. You cannot call yourselves humble, for this does not come from humility.

Sometimes thinking that you are wicked may be humility and virtue, and at other times it may be a great temptation. If we realize our wickedness and that we deserve to be in hell and are upset by our sinfulness, our true humility will be accompanied by an inner peace and joy. It does not upset the soul but enlarges it so it may serve God better. The other kind of distress only upsets and disturbs the mind. The devil is anxious for us to believe that we are humble so he can lead us to distrust God.

If you find yourselves in this state, stop thinking about how worthless you are and start thinking about God's mercy and about His love and sufferings for us. If your state of mind comes from temptation, you will not be able to do this, for you will not be able to calm your mind or to fix your thoughts on anything. This is what happens when we perform excessive penances in order to make ourselves believe that, because of our actions, we are more repentant than others. If we conceal our penances, or if we are told to give them up and do not do so, this is a clear case of temptation. Always be obedient, even when it hurts you to do so, for that is the greatest possible perfection.

Another kind of dangerous temptation often comes our way. Sometimes we feel secure that we will never again return to our past faults or to the world's pleasures. "I know all about these things now," we say, "and I realize that they all come to an end and I get more pleasure from the things of God." This is a dangerous temptation for new Christians. Having this sense of security, they often run again into occasions of sin. They often are so challenged by these occasions that God must preserve them from falling back further than before. No matter how many pledges of love that the Lord gives you, you must never be so sure of yourselves that you stop being afraid of falling back again. You must stay away from opportunities to sin.

Always discuss these graces with someone who can give you light. No matter how sublime your contemplation may be, begin and end every period of prayer with self-examination. If such grace comes from God, you will do this frequently, for such grace brings humility with it and leaves us with more light by which we may see our own unworthiness.

What can we do, Eternal Father, but to run to You and beg You not to allow our enemies to lead us into temptation? If the attacks are made publicly, we will overcome them easily with Your help. How can we be prepared for these treacherous assaults? We must constantly pray for Your help. Show us, Lord, some way of recognizing them and guarding against them. You know that there are very few of us who walk along this road. There will be fewer on this road if they must confront so many fears.

Don't be afraid to walk on these roads, for there are many of them in the life of prayer. Some people get help by using one road and some people get help by using another. This road is a safe one, and you will more readily escape temptation if you are near the Lord than if you are far away from Him. Ask this of God, as you do so many times each day in the Paternoster.

40

Take this advice from your Master. Strive to walk with love and fear, and I guarantee your safety. Love will quicken your steps; fear will make you look where you are stepping so that you do not fall. If we have these two things, we will not be deceived.

Those who really love God love all good, seek all good, help foster all good, and join forces with good people and help and defend them. They love only truth and things worthy of love. Do you think it is possible that anyone who really and truly loves God can love riches and worldly pleasures? Can she engage in strife or feel envy? Her only desire is to please the Beloved. Such people die with longing for Him to love them, so they will give their lives to learn how they may better please Him. Will they hide their love? They cannot do so if their love for God is genuine. Think of Saint Paul or the Magdalen. Saint Paul discovered in three days he was sick with love. The Magdalen discovered this on the very first day. There are degrees of love for God, which shows itself in proportion to its strength. If there is only a little love, it does not show itself very much. If there is a great deal of love, it shows itself accordingly. If it is real love for God, it always reveals itself.

The souls of contemplatives have a great deal of love. If they didn't have so much, they would not be contemplatives. Their love shows itself plainly and in many ways. Their love is a great fire that cannot fail to give out a very bright light. If they don't have much love, they should proceed cautiously and realize that they have great cause to be afraid. They should try to find out what is wrong with them, say their prayers, walk in humility, and ask the Lord not to lead them into temptation. If they walk humbly and strive to discover the truth, the Lord will be faithful to them. If they submit to the Church's teachings, they have no need to be afraid. Whatever fantasies and illusions the devil may invent, he will at once betray his presence.

If you feel this love for God and this fear, you may go on your way with happiness and tranquility. In order to disturb the soul, the devil will upset it with a thousand false fears. If he cannot win souls, he will at least try to make them lose something.

There are two ways that the devil does this. First, many are afraid of engaging in prayer because they think they will be deceived. He can make those people listen to him. Second, he can persuade many not to approach God because they see that He will talk intimately to sinners. Many souls think He will treat them in a similar way, and they are right. I know many people who were inspired in this way who started the habit of prayer. In a very short time they became truly devout and received great favors from God.

When you see someone to whom the Lord is granting these favors, praise Him fervently. But do not imagine that she is safe; help her with more prayers, for no one can be safe amid the engulfing dangers of this stormy sea. You will not fail to recognize this love wherever you find it, for it cannot be concealed. It is impossible to hide our love even for creatures. The more we try to conceal it, the clearer it is revealed. How could a love like God's be concealed? It is so strong, so righteous, continually increasing and resting upon the firm foundation that is its reward. There can be no doubt about the reality of this reward. It is clear in Our Lord's great sorrows, His trials, the shedding of His blood, and even the loss of His life. There is no doubt about this love. It is indeed love, and deserves that name, of which worldly pleasures have robbed it. Think how different one love must be from the other to those who have experienced both.

I hope God will allow us to experience this before He takes us from this life, for it will be a great thing at the hour of death to know we will be judged by One Whom we have loved above everything else with a passion that makes us entirely forget ourselves. Once we have paid our debts we will be able to walk in safety. We will not be going into a foreign land but into our own country, for it belongs to Him Whom we have loved so truly and Who Himself loves us. His love is greater than all earthly affections because if we love Him, we are sure He loves us too. Remember the great gain that comes from this love as well as the loss we feel if we do not possess it. In that case we will be delivered into the tempter's hands that are so cruel to all that is good and so friendly to all that is evil.

What will happen to the poor soul who falls into these hands after emerging from the pains and trials of death? It will have very little rest! It will be torn to pieces as it goes down to hell. It will meet swarms and great varieties of serpents. The place is dreadful. The lodging is miserable. A spoiled person can hardly spend the night in a bad inn. How will the miserable soul feel when it is condemned to such an inn for eternity? Let us not try to spoil ourselves. Let us praise God and strive to do penance in this life. The death of those who have done penance for all their sins and do not have to dwell in purgatory will indeed be sweet. They may well begin to enjoy glory even in this world, and they will not be afraid but know only peace.

If we do not attain this, let us ask God that if we must suffer pains, we have the hope of emerging from them. Then we will suffer them willingly and lose neither God's friendship nor His grace. May He grant us these in life so that we may not unknowingly fall into temptation.

CHAPTER
4I

I have not said as much as I would like about the love of God. It is delightful to talk about this love of God, but it must be even more delightful to possess it. I hope I will not leave this life until there is nothing in it that I want or until I have forgotten what it is to love anything but You. All love but love of God is false. Unless a building's foundations are steady, the building will not stand.

I now want to say a little about the fear of God. I would like to say a little more about worldly love, since I am such an expert on it, so you may free yourselves from it forever. But I need to talk now about the fear of God.

Those who possess the fear of God are very familiar with it. In most people this fear is not very deep, though. It is only deep in the few people that the Lord has made rich in virtues and whom the Lord has raised up to great heights of prayer in a short time. It grows stronger every day, and then it can be recognized. It turns its back on sin, opportunities for sin, bad company. When the soul attains contemplation, its fear of God is plainly revealed. No matter how closely we watch such people we will not see them becoming careless. The Lord preserves them so that they would not commit one venial sin even to further their own interests, and they fear mortal sin like fire. Let us ask God that temptation may not be strong enough for us to offend Him but that He may send it to us in proportion to the strength He gives us to conquer it. If we keep a pure conscience, we can suffer little or no harm. I hope that this fear will never be taken from us, for it is that fear that keeps us in good standing with the Lord.

It is a great thing not to have offended the Lord so that the servants and slaves of hell may be kept under control. In the end, we all serve Him. The slaves of hell are compelled to do so. We serve Him with our entire heart. If we please Him, the servants of hell will be kept at bay. They will not harm us, no matter how much they lead us into temptation and lay secret snares for us.

Do not neglect this advice until you are so determined not to offend the Lord that you would rather lose a thousand lives than commit one mortal sin and until you are most careful not to commit venial sins. I am referring to sins that are committed knowingly. We all commit sins of omission frequently. It is one thing knowingly to commit a sin after long deliberation and quite another to do it so suddenly that the knowledge of its being a venial sin and its commission are one and the same thing. May God deliver us from any sin that we commit with full knowledge, especially since we are sinning against so great a Lord and realize that He is watching us. It is like saying: "Lord, although this displeases You, I will do it. I know You see it and I know You don't want me to do it. But, even though I understand all this, I would rather follow my desire than Your will." If we commit a sin in this way, our offense is very great.

If you want to gain the fear of God, you must realize how serious it is to offend Him. Think about this constantly so you may keep planting a very wholesome fear of God in your minds. Until you are sure you possess this fear, you need to be careful to avoid all occasions of sin and conversations with people who will not help you get nearer to God. Be careful in all that you do. Bend your will to this fear. Be sure that everything you say is uplifting. Run away from all places where the conversation is not pleasing to God. Much care is needed if this fear of God is to be thoroughly impressed upon the soul. If one has true love, though, such love is acquired quickly. Even a soul that is firmly determined may fall from time to time, for we are weak and cannot trust ourselves. Our confidence must come from God. The Lord will help us, and the habits we have formed will help us not to offend Him. We will be able to walk in holy freedom and be able to associate with anyone, even immoral people. These people will not harm you, if you hate sin. Before we had this true fear of God, worldly people would have helped ruin our souls. Now they will help us to love God more and to praise Him for having delivered us from danger. We will help them to repress their weaknesses because they will restrain themselves in our presence.

I often praise the Lord that merely by her presence, and without speaking, a servant of God frequently prevents people from speaking against Him. Since this servant of God is in a state of grace, this grace must cause her to be respected, for they will not bother her when they know she feels so strongly about giving offense to God. Don't be too strict, though. Sometimes too many scruples can hinder progress in you and others. No person, no matter how good in herself, will lead many souls to God if they see she is so strict and distrustful. Human nature is such that these characteristics will frighten it and lead people to avoid the road you are taking, even if they are sure it is the best one.

Try to be as pleasant as you can without offending God, and try to get along as well as you can with people you have to deal with, so that they will like talking to you and want to follow your way of life and conversation and not be frightened and put off by virtue. We must try hard to be pleasant and to humor the people we deal with in order to make them like us.

God does not pay attention to all the trivial matters that we let bother us. Don't let these things make your courage fade, for if you do you will lose many blessings. Let your intention be upright and your will determined not to offend God. Do not let your soul dwell in seclusion, or, rather than becoming holy, you will develop many imperfections.

With the love and the fear of God we can travel along this road in peace and quiet and not be afraid that we will fall into a pit and never reach our goal. We can never be sure of reaching it, so fear will lead the way and we will not grow careless. As long as we live we must never feel completely safe or we will be in great danger. That was our Teacher's meaning at the end of this prayer when He said these words to His Father: "But deliver us from evil."

CHAPTER

42

I think the good Jesus was right to ask this for Himself, for we know how weary He was when He said to His Apostles: "With desire I have desired to eat with you." From this we can see how tired of living He must have been. Nowadays people are not tired of living even at one hundred years old, but they always want to live longer. Our lives are not so difficult for we do not suffer such trials or poverty that Jesus had to bear. What was His entire life but a continuous death, with the picture of the cruel death He was to suffer always before His eyes? Yet He also witnessed so many offenses being committed against His Father and a great multitude of souls being lost. To any human being full of love, this is a great torment. It must have been a greater torment to the boundless love of the Lord. He was right to ask the Father to deliver Him from so many evils and trials and to give Him rest forever in His Kingdom, of which He was the true heir.

The Lord is asking His Father to deliver us from all evil forever. It is useless for us to think that we can be free from numerous temptations and imperfections in our lives. Whoever believes that she is without sin deceives herself. But if we try to banish bodily ills and trials, isn't it right that we should ask to be delivered from sin?

I ask you, Lord, to deliver me from all evil forever, since I cannot pay what I owe and may run further into debt each day. The hardest thing to bear, Lord, is that I cannot know whether or not my desires are acceptable in Your sight and if I love You. Lord, deliver me from all evil and lead me to that place where all good things can be found. What can we look for on earth when You have given us some knowledge of the world and some knowledge of the kind of things the Eternal Father has stored up for us?

When contemplatives ask for this with fervent desire and full determination, it is a clear sign that their contemplation is genuine and the favors they receive in prayer are from God. Let those who receive these favors prize them highly. It is not surprising that those who share God's favors want to go on to a life where they no longer enjoy mere sips of those favors. They do not want to remain in a place where there are so many obstacles to the enjoyment of so many blessings. They do not want to be where the Sun of justice never sets. Anyone who has been given the Kingdom of God on earth must live to do the will of the King.

How much different that life in which we no longer desire death must be. How differently will we bend our wills toward God's will. His will is for us to desire truth, whereas we desire falsehood. His will is for us to desire the eternal, whereas we prefer that which passes away. His will is for us to desire great and sublime things, whereas we desire the sordid things of this world. He would have us desire only what is certain, while here on earth we love what is doubtful. We must ask God to deliver us from these dangers forever and to keep us from all evil. Although we may not have the perfect desire for this, let us strive to make the petition. What does it cost us to ask of One Who is so powerful? Since we have already given Him our will, let us leave the giving to His will, so that we may be more surely heard. May His name be forever hallowed in the Heavens and on earth, and may His will be forever done in me.

You see now what perfection in vocal prayer means. We think about and know to Whom the prayer is being made, Who is making it, and what is its object. No one can deprive you of vocal prayer or make you say the Paternoster hurriedly, without understanding it. If anyone tries to do so, or advises you to give up prayer, pay no attention. If you have learned how to say the Paternoster well, you will know enough to enable you to say all the other vocal prayers you might have to recite.

The Lord has taught us how much we ask for when we repeat this evangelical prayer. May He be forever blessed, for I had not thought about the great secrets that were in it. You have now seen that it comprises the entire spiritual road, right from the beginning, until God absorbs the soul and gives it abundant drink from the fountain of living water at the end of the road. The Lord's will is to teach us what great consolation is contained in it. If you understand the prayer, you will derive a great deal of wisdom from it and it will comfort you.

As we repeat the Paternoster, let us delight in it and strive to learn from so excellent a Master the humility with which He prays. May our Lord forgive me for having dared to speak of such high matters. Our Lord knows well that if He had not taught me what to say, I would not have been capable of understanding this prayer.

Our Lord seems not to want me to write anymore. Although I had intended to go on, I can think of nothing to say. The Lord has shown you the road and has taught me what I wrote in this book. This tells you how to conduct yourselves when you reach this fountain of living water and what the soul experiences there as well as how God quenches the soul's thirst for worldly things and makes it grow in God's service. This will help those who have reached this fountain, and will give them a great deal of light.

Blessed and praised be the Lord, from Whom comes all the good that we speak and think and do. Amen.